Purer in Heart

Heather Pryor

Pryor Convictions Media
St. Petersburg, FL

Pryor Convictions Media exists to provide faith-building materials to home-schools, families and churches. For more information about our other products and publications please visit our website:
www.pryorconvictions.com

or contact us at:
paulpryor@pryorconvictions.com

Table of Contents

How to Use This Book

There are 13 lessons in this book which can be used for personal study or group study. Each lesson contains the lesson portion with scripture readings and questions interspersed. At the end of the lesson, there are thought/discussion questions, a challenge, a prayer request, and a scripture to be committed to memory. These are all designed to further enhance the study and make it personally applicable.

If you are using this book in a group study, it would be ideal for each participant to have a copy of the book in order to read and study the lesson before each class. During the class session, the main ideas of each lesson should be discussed, selected scriptures from the lesson be read aloud, and relevant questions asked and answered both from the lesson portion as well as the thought/discussion section at the end.

Whether this is used as a personal or group study, please go to the Father in prayer as you begin each lesson asking Him to open your heart to His Word. May God bless you as you study and grow in your desire to be purer in heart.

Introduction

In April 2011, my daughter participated in a Purity Banquet which was held by our Keepers at Home Girls Club. My good friend Angela and I were the co-leaders of the club and co-organizers of this banquet. It was a beautiful, memorable event. All of the participating girls wore white gowns. They were presented with white roses from their mothers and they had purity rings placed on their fingers by their fathers after they took a vow of purity before the Lord and witnesses. This vow was not only a vow to remain pure in body for their future husbands, but it was also a vow to remain pure to the Lord in their bodies, minds, and souls. In preparation for this event, we studied a series of lessons on purity with the girls at our club meetings during the months leading up to the banquet. It was important to stress to them that they needed to be pure in *every* area of their lives if they were to be pleasing to God.

The lessons in this book are based on the lessons we taught the girls and ourselves as well. The subject of purity is so important to study, for it is the pure in heart who will one day see God. (Matthew 5:8) Therefore, it should be everyone's desire to refine every area of our lives so that we may all be purer in heart.

"Who may ascend into the hill of the Lord? Or who may stand in His holy place?

He who has clean hands and a pure heart..."

~Psalm 24:3,4

Lesson 1: The Purpose of Purity

How would you describe something that is pure?_____

_____

Perhaps you think of something that is clean and bright, something dazzling white, radiant and spotless without any dark spots or blemishes of any kind.

Advertisers successfully use the word "pure" in their slogans because of the perception we have of it. We assume if the advertised product is as pure as it claims to be, then it must not have anything bad, unclean, or impure in it and therefore, is good! How many of the following claims have you read or heard in advertising: "This laundry detergent will make your sheets and towels pure white"; "Pure, sparkling spring water"; "Pure blend"; "100% pure vegetable oil". These are just some of the common descriptions that we see and hear frequently in advertising...and they are effective.

I remember an occasion when my mother was drinking a glass of water and my uncle kept picking up her glass and sipping on it. My mother loves my uncle, but there are some things not to be shared and her glass of water was one of them. She finally went to the kitchen, drew him his own glass of water from the tap, and proceeded to set it down in front of him. He picked up the glass, held it up to the light, and said, "This water has impurities in it!" then immediately picked up my mother's glass of water again to take a sip. My uncle is a practical joker so we all had a good laugh over his teasing of my mother, but the point is this: if we have a choice between something we perceive to be pure and something we perceive to be impure, the choice is pretty clear, isn't it?

We understand the importance of purity in products such as water and other items like gold although we may not realize or appreciate what processes they undergo in order to make the claim that they are pure.

Pure Gold

Gold goes through an interesting process to receive the label of "pure." In the final steps of gold production, it goes through a refining stage. The gold is liquefied in a furnace and borax and soda ash are added to the molten metal. This process removes any impurities from the gold by separating the pure gold from any other metals and the result is a product that is usually 99.9% pure.[1]

Karatage refers to how much gold is actually

---

1 www.howstuffworks.com

in an item. You have probably seen gold jewelry that is stamped with "14K", "18K", or even "24K". The lower the karatage number, the lower the percentage of gold in that item. For example, a piece of jewelry that is 12 karat gold has only 50% gold in it while a 24 karat gold piece of jewelry has 100% gold content. Items that are pure gold are very soft and pliable while items that have less gold in them are alloyed with other metals to harden the item. So the purest gold is the softest. If our hearts are 100% pure before God, they will be soft and yielding to His touch and His will. However, if we allow impurities to come into our hearts, they will only serve to harden it and make it unyielding to God.

The What and Why of Purity

In order to be purer in heart, we must first understand exactly what purity is and the necessity of it in our lives. "Purity is being chaste, spotless, clean, free from taint or impurity."[2] Think again of the gold illustration, pure gold is just that: gold. Everything else that is not gold is considered impure and has been removed so the gold is free from taint. If our hearts truly belong to God they should be full of Him and everything else that is worldly, fleshly, and sinful is a taint and impurity that must be removed.

Read I John 3:3 and write it here. _____

_____

_____

2 www.dictionary.com

Read Leviticus 11:44-45 and I Peter 1:16. These passages give us the reason why we are to be pure. God is holy and pure, therefore, we as His people must purify ourselves and be holy.

It is vital that we understand the full impact of that last statement. One of the titles of God found in the Old Testament is "the Holy One of Israel." This specific title is used 34 times throughout the Old Testament with 27 of those uses being contained in the book of Isaiah. Isaiah recognized and emphasized the holiness of God as one of His most important characteristics.

Read Isaiah 6:1-7. How does Isaiah describe the Lord as He is seated on His throne?_____

_____

What were the heavenly beings crying out to each other concerning the Lord God? _____

_____

As Isaiah witnessed this vision, he keenly felt the stark contrast of the purity and holiness of God versus his own sinfulness. He laments in Isaiah 1:5, *"Woe is me, for I am undone! Because I am a man of unclean lips, and I dwell in the midst of a people of unclean lips; for my eyes have seen the King, the Lord of hosts."* But Isaiah was not without hope. In verse 7, the seraphim which touched Isaiah's mouth with the coal told him that his sin had been purged. Isaiah was forgiven and his heart cleansed. He was able to stand in the presence of a holy God.

Creating a Pure Heart

Maybe we feel like Isaiah - "Woe is me!" We have the desire to be holy before God, but we are struggling with uncleanness in our hearts. Where do we even begin to start the purifying process? Let's look at the example of David who desired a clean and pure heart and was willing to take the necessary steps to purge the impurities.

Read Psalm 51. Write verse 10 on the lines.

_____

_____

David wrote the 51st Psalm after he was confronted regarding his sin of adultery with Bathsheba. He felt the weight, the guilt, and the filthiness of his sin. He rightly cried out to the One who could lift the burden of the weight from his shoulders, remove the guilt, and wash him clean. Over and over again, David asked to be washed, to be clean so he could be like what? **Read Psalm 51:7.** _____

_____

This verse paints another word picture of purity for us. More than anything, David wanted a clean, pure heart so that he could once again stand before the Lord and have a right relationship with Him.

David is often referred to as "a man after God's own heart". We can look at that description in two different ways: 1) David was a godly man who worked diligently to have a heart like God, and 2) David went after or pursued the heart of God. He always wanted to be in a right relationship with God and be close to Him. David had a soft and yielding heart before His heavenly Father. That is our first step as well in cleansing our hearts from impurities; that is, to go to the One who can truly make us clean and pure and be willing to yield ourselves to Him.

As you approach the throne of God, try praying some of the words of the Psalms as you ask for cleansing from sin. The 51st psalm is a great source for this. *"Have mercy upon me, O God, according to Your lovingkindness."* (verse 1) *"Wash me thoroughly from my iniquity, and cleanse me from my sin."* (verse 2) *"Wash me, and I shall be whiter than snow."* (verse 7b) *"Create in me a clean heart, O God, and renew a steadfast spirit within me."* (verse 10) *"Restore to me the joy of Your salvation, and uphold me with Your generous Spirit."* (verse 12)

While there is certainly nothing wrong with praying the words, "Forgive me of my sins," we run the risk of it becoming less meaningful to us if we just say it by rote and are not careful to concentrate on the full impact of the words. Changing our prayer vocabulary and praying the words of the Psalms can help us to sharpen our focus on the seriousness of sin and our great need for forgiveness from the only One who has the power to cleanse us.

Refined by Fire

Sometimes we will go through a refining process like gold in order to remove impurities. **Read I Peter 1:6-7.** How is gold refined? _____ How is our faith refined and found pure and honorable? Many times, it is through fire as well. Trials by fire can be painful and hard to bear. While going through them, we may wonder if there will ever be light at the end of the tunnel. Will the pain ever end? Will it be worth it to make it through? The answer is "Yes!" It can be a time of fruitfulness if we will let it. Just as the fire purifies the gold by removing any trace of taint, our trials can serve to purify our faith and bring honor and glory to God. Let's take a look at two Biblical examples of trial by fire: 1) Shadrach, Meshach and Abednego, and 2) Job.

Shadrach, Meshach and Abednego were three young men who endured a fiery trial – literally. In Daniel chapter 3, Shadrach, Meshach, and Abednego were three Jewish captives living in the Babylonian empire under the rule of King Nebuchadnezzar. The king built a statue of gold over 90 feet tall, set it up on the plain of Dura, and commanded everyone to bow down before it and worship at the sound of music playing. If anyone was not in compliance with the king's command, they would be thrown in a fiery furnace. Shadrach, Meshach, and Abednego seemed to be in a difficult situation. They were faithful to the one true God and had no intention of worshiping an idol.

On the other hand, disobedience to the powerful king meant certain death. Would their faith withstand this trial? As the sound of trumpets, horns, and harps filled the air, there was a collective dropping to the ground by all of the people standing in the plain of Dura – all that is, except for three young men who refused to disobey their God. Nebuchadnezzar was enraged at their defiance of his command and ordered his furnace to be heated seven times hotter than usual. **Read Daniel 3:16-18.** How did these three young men respond to King Nebuchadnezzar? _____

_____

_____

They boldly proclaimed to the king that either the God of heaven would deliver them from the fiery furnace or He would deliver them from the hand of the king. Either way, they were saved. Shadrach, Meshach, and Abednego were bound hand and foot and tossed in the fiery furnace fully clothed and wearing their hats, but they did not fear what would happen. I often wonder if the words of Isaiah 43:1-3 filled their hearts and minds through this ordeal. **Read Isaiah 43:1-3.** Verse 1 contains the comforting words, *"Fear not...I have called you by name, you are mine."* The latter part of verse 2 states, *"When you walk through the fire, you shall not be burned, nor shall the flame scorch you."* And why would that be? As verse 3 begins, *"For I am the Lord your God, The Holy One of Israel, your Saviour..."* Shadrach, Meshach, and Abednego trusted in their Lord and

Savior and had faith that He could deliver them from the fire unharmed if He so chose and He did. We too can take comfort in the words of God when we are suffering our own fiery trials and use them as anchors for our souls.

Read Daniel 3:27. Not only did the Lord save them, but when the king ordered them to be brought out of the furnace, they had no scorch marks anywhere on their person, and they didn't even smell of smoke!

Standing up for what was right in the face of death would not have been easy, but their faith was strong *before* this incident took place; how much stronger do you think it was *after* this trial by fire? Not only did this trial purify and strengthen their own faith, it glorified God and brought praise and honor to Him. **Read Daniel 3:28-29.** What effect did this event have on king Nebuchadnezzar? _____

_____

_____

Job serves as another example of refining by fire. He was tested in a way that no one else has probably ever experienced. **Read Job chapters 1 and 2** and list all of the calamities that befell him. _____

_____

_____

_____

Why did all of this happen? What kind of man was Job? **Read Job 1:1 and 1:8.** How is Job described? _____

_____

For someone who was so faithful to God, it may be puzzling as to why he suffered so much, but the Bible gives us the answer. **Read Job 1:6-12 and 2:1-7.** Who was behind the suffering of Job? _____
God allowed Satan to test Job because *the Lord knew Job's heart.* God knew that Job could withstand this tremendously difficult refining process and would pass the test. Job, however, did not know why all of this was happening or who was behind it. His friends were accusing him of sin and strongly urging him to repent so that Job's anguish (and seeming punishment) would end. Job acknowledged that he would gladly do so if he was actually guilty of sin, but he knew his heart was pure and blameless before God. **Read Job 23:10.** Job thought the Lord was testing him for some reason that he couldn't understand, but he was confident in the outcome. What did Job say he would come forth as?

_____

We have a behind-the-scenes look into Job's life through the scriptures to understand exactly why all of this happened, but Job never knew why his suffering occurred. What was important to him was to maintain his integrity before God – no matter what. Job boldly stated in Job 23:11-12, *"My foot has held fast to His steps; I have kept His way and not turned aside. I have not departed from the commandment of His lips; I have treasured the words of His mouth more than my necessary food."*

> Trial by fire will produce one of two results: 1) One will in anger and despair turn away from God, or 2) One will hold fast to Him as his rock and fortress and in the process, grow in faith by leaps and bounds.

We don't always know the why's of our suffering and trials, but we can be assured of the faithfulness of God and the outcome of a strong, pure faith if we endure.

Conclusion

Understanding what purity is, the purpose of it in our lives, and going through refining when necessary are the first steps to truly growing purer in heart.

For Thought or Discussion:

1. How do you picture something that is described as pure?

2. Why is a refining process necessary for gold?

3. Why is a refining process sometimes necessary for our faith?

4. What strengthens your faith in times of trial?

5. Look up every use of the title "the Holy One of Israel" in the book of Isaiah.

6. What are the different ways David asks for a pure heart in Psalm 51?

7. How do the words of Isaiah 43:1-3 comfort and encourage you?

8. Besides the fiery furnace, what other historical events or examples in scripture does the Isaiah 43:1-3 passage bring to mind?

9. Why is purity so necessary?

Challenge:

Have a heart of pure gold! Examine it closely and honestly to see if there are any impurities that need to be removed. Target the areas of your life that you need to change and set goals to clean up those spots in your heart. Work diligently to refine your heart so it will be free from all taint and be soft and yielding to God. If you are going through a fiery trial, look to the examples of others who successfully endured and strengthened their faith in the process.

Prayer Request:

Ask the Lord for wisdom and willingness as you examine your heart and determine to remove any spot or blemish in it. Pray for the strength that only He can give to help you overcome any difficulties you face in the refining process. Pray some of the words in the psalms of David as you ask God for a clean heart.

Commit to Memory:

"And everyone who has this hope in Him purifies himself, just as He is pure." ~I John 3:3

Lesson 2: A Special Treasure

When you were a little girl, did you ever dream about being a princess? Maybe you even dressed up like a princess wearing a beautiful dress, a tiara on your head and pretending to live in a lavish castle somewhere far away. Do dreams come true? Well, you may not have married a royal prince and actually moved into a beautiful palace complete with carriages and servants, but guess what? You are a daughter of *The* King, which makes you a princess! Take a minute and let the impact of that fully sink in...

Royal Behavior

Many years ago there was a movie about a teenaged girl who lived an ordinary life – going to school, hanging out with her friends, wearing T-shirts and jeans and chewing bubble gum. Her world is instantly turned upside down when she discovers that she is actually the heir apparent to the throne of a small remote country she's never heard of. She is whisked away to live in a castle and is suddenly surrounded by servants, social occasions and sermons. Not sermons from a preacher, but rather, she has to constantly be taught and trained as to the proper behavior and protocol of a princess. Princesses are, after all, expected to behave in a certain manner. Hilarity ensues as she awkwardly tries to make the transition from an average American teenager to sophisticated, genteel royalty.

So, how is a princess to behave? What constitutes "acceptable" royal behavior for her? There are, of course, the obvious rules of good manners and civility and graciousness in speaking to people. There are also certain protocols as to receiving guests, dining, and speaking engagements. In short, we would say that a princess behaves graciously, properly, humbly, and decently.

A princess is expected to be modest in her appearance and manner. She does not do anything outrageous, outlandish or rude, does not draw any undue or negative attention to herself, and she is certainly *never* to do anything that would bring shame or disgrace on her father, the King.

Read II Corinthians 6:18 and write it on the lines.

_____

_____

_____

The Lord God Almighty, King of heaven above, earth beneath, and the entire universe has said that we are His daughters – we are princesses. How should that remarkable fact cause us to behave? _____

_____

_____

_____

The Kingship of God

Throughout history, we see the stories of many kings. Some were rich and powerful, some were weak. Some ruled over a vast empire and some only controlled a small geographical area, but all of these monarchs had characteristics in common. What are some of the characteristics of a king?

- *He is a ruler.* The title of king implies that he has a kingdom to rule over. He reigns over a number of subjects whether few or many.

- *He has authority.* His subjects are just that: subject to the king's wants and wishes because he has the authority to command.

- *He is respected and served.* His very title commands respect and obedience from all of his subjects. Even those outside of his realm pay him proper respect when they visit his kingdom.

Of all the kings that ever lived and reigned upon the earth, King Solomon exceeded them all. In terms of riches, honor, glory, peace and prosperity, there has not been a king to rival him, but even Solomon pales in comparison to the one King who is above all kings.

The Bible has much to say about the Kingship of God. Read the following verses and write down how God is described as King or what He does as King:

- **Psalm 103:19** _____

  _____

- **Exodus 15:18** _____

  _____

- **I Chronicles 29:11-12** _____

  _____

- **Psalm 47:8** _____

  _____

- **Daniel 2:21** _____

  _____

- **Psalm 29:10** _____

  _____

- **Daniel 4:25** _____

  _____

We clearly see from these verses that the Lord is the one true King over all with all authority, might, and majesty who reigns forever and ever. When we understand the Kingship of God, it will impact our hearts to demonstrate all of the qualities of purity and holiness that are characteristic of His royal daughters.

Queen Esther

In the book of Esther we read of a young Jewish woman, orphaned and in exile, who was unexpectedly thrust into the role of queen of the mighty Persian empire. Her story is a great favorite among girls, especially because it is the true adventure of a life that most girls can only dream of. Unlike the fairy tale of Cinderella where an unlikely, lowly girl is chosen to be queen and lives happily ever after in her castle, Esther's story wasn't a fairy tale and everything wasn't "happily ever after" for her after being chosen queen. Esther's life wasn't just remarkable for her rise to royalty but for first and foremost behaving as a royal daughter of the one true King.

Read Esther 1-4. These chapters lay the groundwork for Esther's opportunity to become queen of the Persian empire as well as highlight some of the beautiful qualities she possessed.

Let's take a closer look at some of the characteristics of Esther. **Read Esther 2:2.** One of the qualifications the king had for his new queen was that she must be a virgin. Esther fulfilled this requirement as she was chaste and pure in her body. She was a virgin that had never compromised her purity by sharing any part of her body with a man. This would also imply that she was modest in her dress and her behavior towards men.

Read Esther 2:7. How is Esther described?

_____

_____

Esther was a beautiful and lovely young woman. You may have heard the saying that beauty is only skin deep. In other words, the outer beauty doesn't go very far if there is no inner beauty. You may have experienced this if you have known women or girls who were gorgeous on the outside but so ugly on the inside that it actually diminished their outward looks. On the other side of that coin, you may have known women or girls who were not especially attractive on the outside but had such a beautiful spirit that it actually enhanced their outward appearance. Esther, it would seem, was blessed with beauty both inside and out.

Read Esther 2:15, 17. Whom did she obtain favor with? _____

_____

People genuinely liked Esther for who she was as a person. She had a personality and demeanor which caused everyone who came in contact with her to like her and enjoy being around her. It was an admirable and pleasing quality which caused her to stand out from the crowd.

Read Esther 2:20. Even after being chosen queen of the Persian empire, Esther remained obedient to Mordecai, the man she looked to as a father. **Read Ephesians 6:1-3.** As single girls, we are commanded to honor and obey our parents, being humbly submissive to their authority. **Read Ephesians 5:22-23 and I Peter 3:1,6.** As married women, whom do we honor, obey, and submit to? _____
Esther didn't chafe at being obedient to her father figure but lovingly respected him and acted as a dutiful daughter. This shows us Esther's heart of humility.

Read Esther 4:1-4. Esther was compassionate and generous. When she knew that Mordecai was in distress and sorrow, she did what she could to try to cheer him and help him. What did she attempt to do for Mordecai in these verses? _____

_____

Read Esther 4:13-16. What question did Mordecai ask Esther? _____

_____

_____

When the Jews were threatened with annihilation in the Persian empire, Mordecai pleaded with Esther to use her position as queen to help deliver her people. Esther was faced with a difficult choice since going before the king without permission could have meant her death according to the law of the Persians, but Esther was a woman of courage. She did what was right even though it was potentially dangerous and frightening. How was she able to do this? She was a woman of faith. Mordecai's words must have echoed in her mind over and over: *"Who knows whether you have come to the kingdom for such a time as this?"* She realized that she wasn't just lucky to have won the beauty pageant and been chosen queen. It was not a coincidence; it was the hand of God. She was in the place and position that God wanted her to be in order to do His will and it was accomplished through her, His royal daughter.

Characteristics of a Daughter of the King

Esther possessed some sterling qualities that modeled what true royal behavior looks like, qualities that each of us should try to imitate. Let's review the seven characteristics that Esther possessed:

1. *Modest and pure*

2. *Inner beauty*

3. *Pleasant personality*

4. *Obedient and submissive*

5. *Compassionate and generous*

6. *Courageous*

7. *Faithful*

> Being royalty is more than playing dress-up and wearing a crown; it is a life of commitment to a royal standard – God's standard.

We may not be the queen of a vast empire as Esther was, but we are daughters of *the* King, and therefore, must strive to possess these same qualities. They are all characteristics which God the Father desires His daughters to possess and put into practice.

Chosen and Special

Read I Peter 2:9 and write it here.

_____

_____

_____

_____

So many in our world today suffer from low self-esteem. They may feel unloved, of no particular value, and certainly not special. Maybe they have an earthly father who was unkind or cruel, or worse yet, one who abandoned them altogether. If only everyone would read this verse and take it to heart! Look again at the words Peter uses to describe what you are:

chosen, royal, holy, special, His own. How does that make you feel? _____

_____

_____

Read Exodus 19:5. God's people were called *"a special treasure."* If someone is chosen and special, how are they treated? _____

_____

_____

God treats us with the tender-loving care and the fierce protection of a Father whose child is the apple of His eye. (Zechariah 2:8) But notice that Exodus 19:5 contains an "if, then" statement. God will treat His people as a special treasure, *if* His people will do what?

_____

_____

_____

Conclusion

Our heavenly Father will always love us, even when we disappoint or disgrace Him, but His great delight is in our obedience to Him in all things. You are a treasured possession to your Father the King when your purity shines like the sun before Him. Never forget for one moment who you are: you are a special treasure - you are a daughter of *the* King.

<u>For Thought or Discussion</u>:

1. Write some of the descriptions and characteristics of the Kingship of God.

2. How should a princess behave?

3. What seven characteristics did Esther possess?

4. In what ways did she find favor with those around her? How can we imitate that today?

31

5. As daughters of the King, how should we behave?

6. Why do you think so many people have low self-esteem? How does being a child of God change the way we look at ourselves?

7. What does Zechariah 2:8 say?

8. How does Exodus 19:5 motivate you to be obedient to your heavenly Father?

Challenge:

Examine the behavior in your life and honestly assess whether it is how a daughter of the King should act. If not, be willing to make the necessary changes to live your life in such a way that you will not bring shame on your Father, the King. Place a small crown sticker in a place where you will see it often to remind you who you are and to encourage you to live up to a royal standard – God's standard.

Prayer Request:

Pray to your Father, the King, to help you live a life that is pleasing to Him as His daughter. Ask Him to help you manifest the characteristics of modesty, purity, inner beauty, a pleasant personality, obedience, submission, compassion, generosity, courage, and faith in your life as Esther did.

Commit to Memory:

"Now therefore, if you will indeed obey My voice and keep My covenant, then you shall be a special treasure to Me above all people; for all the earth is Mine." ~Exodus 19:5

Lesson 3: Purity In Our Speech

You may remember the words of a children's song often sung in Sunday school which say, "Oh, be careful little mouth what you say." The song emphasizes the importance of watching what we say as well as everything we do because "the Father up above is looking down in tender love." He is watching – and listening – to everything.

Impure Speech

We might tend to think of impure speech as cursing or talking dirty, and while those certainly qualify as such, impure speech encompasses much more than that. If our speech is to be pure, then it must be free from anything that would be considered a taint. Remember the illustration of pure gold? It is not able to be called "pure" unless every impurity and taint is removed. Let's consider some scriptures that give examples of several types of impure speech. Read each of the following verses and list the unacceptable speech that is described:

- **James 3:10** _____
- **Matthew 12:36** _____
- **I Timothy 5:13** _____
- **Philippians 2:14** _____
- **Ephesians 4:26** _____

Let's examine each one of these in more detail:

Cursing: This would include any kind of profanity or swearing but would also include speaking a wish of harm or evil to come upon someone.

Idle, vain words: Vain words have no worth, value, or importance. They are shallow and useless.

Gossip: Gossip, or talebearing, is the spreading of lies or false accusations against someone. It is described as "running from house to house" to "tattletale". Even if the report being spread is true, telling it to others is harmful and destructive. (Proverbs 11:13)

Complaining: Complaining encompasses fault-finding, lamenting, whining, impatience, and ingratitude.

Angry words: God created us to have emotions and anger is certainly one of them. However, the Bible is clear that we are not to sin in our anger. Psalm 4:4 tells us, *"Be angry and do not sin."* This includes saying words in anger that would wound and cause damage.

This hits a little closer to home, doesn't it? We may not have any problem with talking dirty or cursing, but gossip, complaining, vain words? Ouch! From these scriptures, we can clearly see several kinds of speech that are unacceptable to our Lord, but there are still more.

Read Proverbs 6:16-19. Out of the seven things listed which are an abomination to the Lord, three of them involve the words we speak! Lying, being a false witness against someone, and sowing discord among the brethren all involve using our words. How does verse 16 describe these seven sins? _____
The word *abomination* is one which indicates strong loathing and disgust. That is exactly how the Lord feels about a lying tongue and hateful, spiteful words that cause division in the church. So, does it matter if we tell a "little white lie"? Absolutely!

Another area of speech that we should consider is crude/vulgar speech. In our first lesson, we discussed the holiness of God. Remember how Isaiah declared he was a man of unclean lips as he witnessed God's purity as King? In our last lesson, we discussed appropriate royal behavior for daughters of The King. Keeping those things in mind, picture a princess hosting a dinner party at the royal palace and blurting out, "Oh, cr*p!" as she accidentally drops her fork on the floor. Or can you imagine that princess sharing graphic, personal details about her monthly cycle or other bodily functions with the other ladies seated around her? I think it is safe to say that would go against royal protocol. Why? Because it is not ladylike or appropriate. My purpose is not to publish a "banned word/topics list". However, I would like each of us to consider carefully the words that we speak, measuring them for purity, holiness, and appropriateness. Ladies, let's be careful that we're not relaxing (or reducing) our standards to talking like the world around us. Let's speak like the ladies God created us to be. If our speech is exactly the same as the world around us, then the world will not see Christ living in us. One of the defining factors of a Christian life is that we are distinctly different from the world, and one of the areas where the world recognizes that the most is in our speech.

Read Proverbs 30:5a. How is every word of God described in this verse? _____ If we are to be holy as God is holy, then we can do no less than to use pure, wholesome words. If you honestly want to know if certain words are appropriate, ask yourself the following questions:

1) Would the Lord consider these words holy and pure and have used them when He spoke to others while here on earth?

2) Would you use these words in prayer as you are talking to the Most Holy God?

One more area of speech that we need to consider carefully is euphemisms. What is a euphemism? _____

_____

Many times we substitute one word or phrase for another because we think it's "nicer" or more acceptable, but I challenge you to prayerfully consider if it is pure, God-honoring speech. For example, we may use words like "darn", "heck", or "geez", but what are we substituting them for and the bigger question is why? Some may answer, "Well, I have to say *something*!" Do we? Remember that one of the categories of unacceptable speech was vain, idle words. If we are saying words of no worth or value, such as euphemisms, then we need to work on eliminating them from our vocabulary.

Read Matthew 12:36 What did Jesus say we will give an account for?_____
Jesus said that on judgment day, people will have to answer for **every idle word** spoken. That is something to think seriously about.

Controlling Our Tongue

Our tongue is actually one of the hardest things for us to control. The irony is that it is such a little part of our body and yet it wields great power.

Read James 3:1-12. James talks about two relatively small things that control big, powerful things: a bit in a horse's mouth and a rudder of a ship. Horses are extremely powerful animals yet their strength can be reined in and controlled by pulling on the bridle which contains the little bit in their mouth. You can pull the reins left and it pulls the horse's head left which causes him to turn in that direction. Pull straight back on the reins and the horse's head is forced to pull up and he stops. In a similar way, a captain of a ship can turn the rudder and the huge ship will maneuver in whatever direction the captain wishes. Even a great, raging forest fire is sometimes started by just one tiny match. How does James describe the tongue in verse 8? _____

_____

There is potential to do either good or evil with our tongue, but it should not be doing both. Verses 9 and 10 speak of blessing and cursing coming out of the same mouth, blessing God on the one hand and cursing men on the other. James says this should not be. Why? It is evidence of an impure heart. Jesus said in Matthew 12:34b, *"For out of the abundance of the heart the mouth speaks,"* so if we have a heart that is not pure, it will be evident in our speech. To what does James compare good and evil speech coming from the same mouth? _____

_____

Paul echoes a similar thought as he phrases it this way in Ephesians 5:4, *"Neither filthiness, nor foolish talking, nor coarse jesting, which are not fitting, but rather giving of thanks."*

What are we to put out of our mouth according to **Colossians 3:8**? _____

King David also has this reminder in Psalm 34:13,

"Keep your tongue from evil, and your lips from speaking guile." There is simply no place in the speech of a Christian for unholy talk of any kind.

If you've ever attended a circus or a theme park, you've seen a variety of wild animals being controlled by their trainers from little monkeys and birds to fierce lions and giant killer whales. All of them can be trained and brought under control by people, but people have never been able to master the art of taming their own tongue. It is something that we will have to work on all of our lives. That is why it is so important to taste our talk each day.

Taste Your Talk

Read Psalm 19:14 and write it here. _____

_____

_____

_____

It was important to David that every time he opened his mouth, his words would be God-honoring. He adds in Psalm 51:15, *"O Lord, open my lips, and my mouth shall show forth Your praise."* Purity in our speech is important because *"the words of our mouth"* need to be acceptable to God.

Do you ever taste your talk? That is, do you ever stop to roll your words over your tongue and around in your mouth before you actually say them? It would be a wonderful thing if everyone were to do that! Each of us needs to taste our words to see if they are sweet, sour, or even bitter. Words are powerful, and once they are said, they can never be taken back.

Our words have the power to build up, encourage, cheer, heal, and praise, but they also have the power to discourage, criticize, hurt, and destroy. Considering the power that is contained in our words, we should take great care in choosing them and using them.

Read Proverbs 31:26 and write it here.

_____

_____

_____

One of the many beautiful qualities of the virtuous woman is her kindness of speech. Her words were never harsh or destructive but gentle and uplifting. **Read Ephesians 4:29.** What good does the apostle Paul say our words should be used for? _____ The word edification simply means "building up." Our words should be used as a means of encouragement to others. There is certainly enough "tearing down" that takes place in the world around us. One doesn't have to look far to see hateful, nasty, spiteful words directed at others, maybe even yourself. It is all over the news, television and social media. In view of that, it's like a breath of fresh air to talk to someone who uses pleasant, uplifting words.

Read Colossians 4:6. With what does Paul say our speech should be seasoned? _____

Read Ecclesiastes 10:12. What does Solomon say a wise man's words are?_____

Each of these last few verses deal with our speech giving grace to others or having gracious, kind speech. Again, with so much unkindness, anger and hate in our world, it makes such a noticeable difference when one speaks kindly, gently, and encouragingly. As we taste our talk, let's make sure all of our words taste sweet, kind and gracious. Proverbs 16:24 states, *"Pleasant words are like a honeycomb, sweetness to the soul and health to the bones."*

Read Proverbs 15:26b and write it on the lines.

_____

_____

Words of Wisdom

Solomon had a lot to say about our words and what constitutes wise speech. Look up each of the following scriptures and write a short description of what our words can do.

- **Proverbs 13:3** _____
- **Proverbs 15:1** _____
- **Proverbs 15:23** _____
- **Proverbs 22:11** _____

So careful we must be about the words we say, it even extends to what we say in private when we think no one else hears. **Read Ecclesiastes 10:20.** From this verse we get our saying, "A little bird told me." You never know who may overhear something you say and spread it far and wide. **Read Luke 12:3.** Jesus makes it clear as well that words seemingly spoken in private often do not remain so. **Read Psalm 139:4.** Ultimately, every single word we speak is known to Almighty God. Knowing this, it should truly cause us to "be careful little mouth what we say."

Conclusion

God takes sin seriously and so should we. It is clear from the Scriptures that there are several sins that can be committed with our tongues that we need to be on guard against. Being purer in heart requires us to have pure speech so that the words of our mouth will be acceptable in the sight of God.

For Thought or Discussion:

1. Impure speech encompasses many things. List all of the areas of impure speech that were discussed in this lesson. Can you think of any more to add to the list?

2. What areas of impure speech do you struggle with the most?

3. Contrast the world's view of lying to God's viewpoint of lying.

4. What are some practical things we can do to help us control our tongue?

5. What does it mean to "taste your talk"?

6. What does Jesus say our words will do for us in Matthew 12:37 and how does this emphasize the importance of watching what we say?

Challenge:

Examine your speech – are you in the habit of speaking unkind words, euphemisms, negative words, lies, complaints, or vain words? Challenge yourself to tackle any kinds of speech you know are not acceptable and pure before God and make a conscious effort to change them.

Prayer Request:

Pray for strength in controlling your tongue and using your speech in ways that edify others and glorify God. Pray the words of Psalm 141:3 which say, *"Set a guard, O Lord, over my mouth, keep watch over the door of my lips."*

Commit to Memory:

"For then I will restore to the peoples a pure language, that they all may call on the name of the Lord, to serve Him with one accord." *~Zephaniah 3:9*

Lesson 4: Purity In Our Thoughts

A man and his wife were driving down the road one day when a car suddenly darted out in front of them, causing the man to slam on the brakes to avoid a collision. The car in front sped up and away and the man and his wife resumed their drive with accelerated heart rates. As the wife glanced at her husband, she saw his hands clenching the steering wheel tightly, his brow furrowed and his lips compressed. She ventured, "Boy, that was close! What were you thinking when that car pulled out in front of us?"

"You don't want to know!" he replied.

"Well, I hope you weren't thinking any bad words," she said.

Her husband snapped, "Well, at least I didn't say them out loud!"

No Harm Done?

We each have a secret place, tucked away where

no one else can enter, a place where we can hide things away from the prying eyes of the world. We keep things in the deep, dark recesses of our mind that we believe are locked up safely and that we alone have the key to access them. We think that no matter what we hide there, it's okay as long as we keep it there...We have lulled ourselves into a false sense of security.

How often have we had impure thoughts such as the man above: bad words, mean thoughts about someone, thoughts of vengeance, or thoughts of sinful, ugly things, but we consoled ourselves with the fact that we only thought them but didn't say them out loud or act on them? No harm was actually done because no one knew what we were thinking. Right?

Read Mark 4:22 and write it on the lines.

_____

_____

_____

_____

_____

Is it okay if our impure thoughts remain hidden? The truth is they are not hidden, but they are open before the Lord and will even be used to judge us. **Read Psalm 44:21** and write it here. _____

_____

_____

Ecclesiastes 12:14 states, *"For God will bring every work into judgment, including **every secret thing**, whether it is* *good or whether it is evil."* **Read Hebrews 4:13** and write it here. _____

_____

_____

_____

_____

Luke 8:17 also says, *"For nothing is secret that will not be revealed, nor anything hidden that will not be known and come to light."* Can you imagine what it would be like on judgment day as you are standing before Almighty God with a crowd of people behind you awaiting their turn and the Lord begins to show on a screen every thought you have ever had? One image after another keeps appearing where everybody can see all of the things you have ever thought. Would you cringe in shame and embarrassment to have your secret thoughts revealed? This is why it is so important to have purity in our thoughts; it is an area of our lives that we tend to think of as very private and isolated and therefore, maybe not as carefully regulated.

Evil Thoughts

The Lord recognizes the danger when we harbor sinful thoughts. In fact, in the beginning He had to warn one of His creation about this very thing. **Read Genesis 4:1-5.** Cain and his brother Abel, both presented offerings to the Lord. The Lord was pleased with Abel's offering and accepted it, but He did not find Cain's offering to be acceptable. We are given more insight into this situation in the book of Hebrews. **Read Hebrews 11:4.** How did Abel offer his sacrifice?

_____

Faith was the missing element in Cain's sacrifice. Romans 10:17 tells us, *"So then faith comes by hearing, and hearing by the word of God."* We can put these pieces of the puzzle together to help us see the full picture. Cain and Abel had to have heard what God required of them in order to offer acceptable worship to Him. Abel believed what he heard and acted in obedience. That is, by faith Abel offered his sacrifice. Cain, on the other hand, chose to do it his own way and not according to the word of the Lord. He did not make his offering by faith and therefore, God had no respect for his offering. The fault of Cain's offering not being acceptable to God was no one's fault but Cain's. Yet, Cain was not angry at himself but at his brother Abel. Cain started down the dangerous road of harboring angry, sinful thoughts in the dark corners of his mind probably consoling himself with the fact that his father, mother and brother had no idea what he was thinking. But God knew. **Read Genesis 4:6-7.** What warning did the Lord issue to Cain? _____

_____

The Lord was giving Cain a golden opportunity to purge his mind of the evil that was brewing there. He gave him a chance to avoid acting upon those thoughts and committing a terrible crime. The Lord warned Cain that he was at a fork in the road and he had a serious choice to make. **Read Genesis 4:8.** Sadly, Cain did not make the right choice. He violently acted out his pent-up anger and hatred toward his brother and killed him, thus becoming the first murderer in history.

In the days of Noah, the earth was corrupt and filled with violence. (Genesis 6:11) It had reached a point where the Lord was ready to destroy man whom He had created except for righteous Noah and his family whom He saved in the ark. The Lord sent a global flood which wiped out all living creatures on the face of the earth in a massive destruction, then started afresh with a godly family of eight people. How did things ever reach that point and become so bad? Genesis 6:5 reveals the answer, *"Then the Lord saw that the wickedness of man was great in the earth, and that **every intent of the thoughts of his heart was only evil continually**."* Take a moment to imagine the state of the world in Noah's day. What would that world look like where everyone only thought evil continually? No wonder Genesis 6:11 describes it as a world *"corrupt and filled with violence."*

Read and write Matthew 15:19. _____

_____

_____

_____

51

Where do sinful, violent, and vile actions come from? They start in heart with the thoughts we think. The people in Noah's day were acting out the sinful thoughts of their hearts which they were thinking continually. Once there is no safeguard in place to keep our thoughts under control and pure before the Lord, then there is no stopping the resulting actions from those thoughts as we have seen with Cain and the people of Noah's day. So what do we do about impure thoughts? How do we put the brakes on in our minds to keep ourselves from becoming like the people in Noah's day? Having purity in our thoughts is based on controlling what goes into our mind.

Garbage In, Garbage Out

There used to be a popular computer acronym in the '80's: GIGO, which stood for "Garbage In, Garbage Out". If we continually put garbage in our minds through what we listen to and look at, then we can't expect to manifest anything but garbage in our lives. The converse is also true: if we put pure, righteous things in our minds, then that is what will show itself in our lives. **Read Proverbs 12:5a** and write it here. _____

_____

King David said in Psalm 101:3a, *"I will set nothing wicked before my eyes,"* but David didn't stop there. He understood that he didn't need to look upon anything that was wicked, but he also understood that there were other things that could be considered "garbage" as well. What did he ask of the Lord in **Psalm 119:37**? _____

_____

Not only do we need to avoid putting wicked things into our minds, but we also need to avoid worthless things. There are numerous worthless things in front of our faces every day in entertainment, social media, and even news and education. We need to filter out the things that are shallow, untruthful, foolish, and a waste of time. These are things not worth looking at or wasting time thinking about especially when there are so many worthwhile things to put into our minds.

Since our thoughts will be based on what we listen to and look at, it should make us take a closer look at our lives and ask ourselves some hard questions.

- Is this song I'm listening to God-honoring or Satan-honoring?

- Is this program I'm watching one that I would be embarrassed to have my children/parents watching with me?

- Would I be looking at these images on my computer/cell phone if my preacher was looking over my shoulder?

- Is this movie that I bought a ticket to, one that I

would be comfortable watching with Jesus sitting next to me?

- Does this joke or comedy routine I'm listening to use language that I would use in front of little children in a Bible class?

- Would I be comfortable with all of my Facebook comments/photos or other social media on the big screen at church on Sunday morning for all to see?

If we answer truthfully, we *do* know what things we should and should not be listening to or looking at and we then need to resolve, like David, to *"set nothing wicked before me."*

We cannot afford to turn loose the reins of our minds and leave them wide open to anything. Satan will be ready and waiting to fill them. Instead, we must actively take control of what we allow into our minds. **Read II Corinthians 10:5.** What are we to do with our thoughts? _____

_____

How many of our thoughts are to be brought captive to the obedience of Christ? Every – single – one.

54

Think On These Things...

What if we have developed the bad habit of looking at and listening to impure things for quite some time? How do we captivate our thoughts and make them obedient to Christ? How do we remove the impure? By replacing it with the pure. You can never remove images and words you already have in your mind, but you can continually crowd them out with pure, good images and words if you'll surround yourself with them.

As far as words go, there is nothing better than to memorize scripture as a pleasurable, pure thing to think on as well as to act as a safeguard against sin. **Read and write Psalm 119:11.** _____

_____

Psalm 1:2 also reminds us, *"But his delight is in the law of the Lord, and in His law he meditates day and night."* There is nothing more pure and lovely to think about than the holy words of the Bible. Work diligently to cultivate a desire and hunger for these words that are so sweet to our souls. **Read and write Psalm 119:103.**

_____

_____

Dedicate yourself to setting aside time each day to memorize and think about scripture. You will be amazed at how many situations you will find yourself in where a certain verse will just pop into your mind serving to encourage and comfort you or to help you fight temptation. It is a blessing and a comfort to hold God's Word close in your heart. **Read Isaiah 26:3a** and write its assuring words on the lines. _____

_____

Here is a helpful acronym of the word "thoughts" to serve as a guideline for the way we should think.

T - Is it True?

H - Does it Honor God?

O - What is its Origin?

U - Is it Uplifting?

G - Does it involve Guilt?

H - Is it Helpful?

T - Is it a Temptation?

S - Does it Strengthen you?

The best guideline for pure thoughts is **Philippians 4:8**. This verse helps us to know if what we are thinking passes the "purity test'. Read it and write it here. _____

_____

_____

_____

_____

_____

This tells us exactly what kinds of things we are to think on so there can be no doubt. If we will try to fill our minds with these things, the result can only be thoughts which are pure, holy, and pleasing to God.

Conclusion

Controlling our thoughts and developing a pure mind are an essential foundation to our lives as Christians. We cannot harbor impurity in our thoughts and expect it to remain hidden and not show itself in outward actions or words at some point. We should strive every day to, *"Let this mind be in you which was also in Christ Jesus."* (Philippians 2:5) To have a Christ-like mind is to have a mind of pure thoughts centered on Him, His word, and His will. Commit yourself to being purer in heart through purity in your thoughts.

For Thought or Discussion:

1. What challenges would Noah and his family have faced in remaining pure of thought?

2. What challenges do we face today in keeping our thoughts pure?

3. What proactive steps can you take to feed your mind pure things?

4. How often do you commit scripture to memory? What steps can you take to make it easier to do this?

5. How does the memorization of scripture act as a safeguard against sin?

6. In Psalm 119:37, David speaks of not looking at "worthless things". What are some specific things that you would describe as worthless to look at?

7. Are there things in your life that need to be removed or replaced because they are tempting you with impure thoughts?

8. Why is purity in our thoughts so vital?

Challenge:

Try turning off the TV and social media for one week. In place of it, see how many books of the Bible you can read through, how many people you can minister to through phone calls, cards, or other acts of encouragement, and how many scriptures you can memorize. Once you've done this, reflect on the state of your thoughts. Are they improved? Do you feel more peaceful? Closer to God?

Prayer Request:

Ask the Lord to help you fill your mind with things that would be pure and pleasing to Him. Pray for strength to rid your mind and heart of things that dishonor Him and ask for His help in committing His precious word to your heart.

Commit to Memory:

"Finally, brethren, whatever things are true, whatever things are noble, whatever things are just, whatever things are pure, whatever things are lovely, whatever things are of good report, if there is any virtue and if there is anything praiseworthy – meditate on these things." ~Philippians 4:8

Lesson 5: Purity In Our Motives

One Sunday morning a woman started visiting a new church. After several weeks went by, she decided she would place membership and become a part of that congregation. She was a woman who was well-off financially, and she wanted to use some of her money to make a substantial contribution to the church. She wrote out her check and gave it to one of the elders. As she handed it over, she told him that she wanted it announced on Sunday morning that she had made a sizable donation to the church. She knew the church building was in need of repairs and that the members would be so grateful to her for her generosity...Is there anything wrong with this picture?

What Motivates You To Do Good?

Why do you do the things you do? Do you expect the pat on the back from everyone? Are you hoping for some kind of recognition or reward? Do you like basking in the sunshine of praise as it beams upon you? Or are you doing good for the sole reason of pleasing the Lord, even if He is the only one who sees what you do?

Pure motives are important to God. It is not just what we do but why we are doing it that matters. If we are not doing good from pure motives, then we may be acting as the hypocrites. Write the definition of a hypocrite. _____

_____

The origin of this word is interesting. Strong's Concordance notes that it comes from the Greek word *hypokrites* which means "stage actor". A hypocrite is someone acting a part, a pretender. Nothing he does or says is from a pure motive but from a false one. In Jesus' Sermon on the Mount, he had a lot to say about the motives of a hypocrite versus the motives of one who is pure in heart. Let's examine three areas He addresses: charitable deeds, prayer, and fasting.

Charitable Deeds

Read Matthew 6:1-4. Jesus discusses doing good deeds for two reasons: 1) The glory of men, and 2) The love of the Father in heaven. He describes the hypocrites doing their good works in such a way that they were sure to draw attention to themselves, like blasting a trumpet. It's as if they were shouting aloud, "Look at me! Look at what I'm doing!" then others would fall all over themselves to praise them to the skies. This happens frequently even today and those people get the reward they are seeking - the praise and glory of men. Jesus then describes the one who does his good deeds for the love of God. How will that person go about doing his good work? _____

_____

_____

Jesus describes it as not even letting your left hand know what your right hand is doing. He is simply emphasizing the point of doing it discreetly. This does not mean that we have to sneak around under cover of darkness to leave a casserole on someone's front porch, then running after ringing the doorbell in order to avoid being seen. It just means that we go about our lives, doing what good works we can and serving where we are able without deliberately drawing attention to ourselves. How does the Lord reward one who does their good deeds in this way?_____

_____

Read Matthew 5:16. Is this a contradiction? How are we to do our good works secretly but also let our light shine by letting others see our good works? There is nothing wrong with others seeing our good works if we are not doing them in order to draw attention to ourselves. It is an opportunity to draw attention to God and to give Him the honor and glory that He is worthy of. Doing good works with the right motivation is putting the spotlight not on ourselves but on God where it belongs.

Prayer

Read Matthew 6:5-15. The second area Jesus

addresses is prayer. He again draws a contrast between the hypocrites and the righteous through the prayers that they offer. How do the hypocrites pray? _____

_____

These prayers are people-pleasing and not God-pleasing. It is yet another opportunity for the hypocrites to toot their own horn and say, "Look at me!" They want to be looked at as so religious and faithful when in reality their hearts are full of selfish pride rather than God. If someone truly wants to talk to His Father in heaven, Jesus says he will do it quietly and sincerely with a heart of faith. Notice in verse 7 that Jesus warns against using "vain repetitions." In a previous lesson, we discussed vain words as being impure speech. Something that is vain is useless and meaningless. Pleasing prayers need to be sincere and meaningful.

Matthew 6:9-13 is often referred to as "The Lord's Prayer." Read it slowly and carefully. **Read Luke 18:11-12**. Let's contrast these two prayers. In the Lord's prayer, Jesus gives us an example of how we should address the Father - in reverence and humility. We are to pray for daily provision and forgiveness, for mercy and grace. In the Pharisee's prayer, he proudly informs God that he is not a miserable sinner like others around him and isn't God lucky to have him? He then gives God his list of all of the good things he does each week. This prayer is an exact opposite to the model Jesus sets forth for us. The Pharisee's prayer contains no reverence or humility. He does not ask God for any kind of care or provision and certainly for no forgiveness. His prayer comes from a puffed-up heart full of pride.

The Lord wants us to pray to Him, but He wants those prayers to come up before Him from a heart that is emptied of self and full of Him.

Fasting

The third area Jesus addresses is fasting. When we think of fasting we tend to think of abstaining from food for a certain amount of time, but fasting could also be giving up anything temporarily in order to focus more of one's attention on God. Fasting in the Bible was usually closely connected with prayer. (Luke 2:37; 5:33) One would fast by giving up something for a short time, such as eating, and diligently devote that time to prayer. Fasting was done for many different reasons. Look up the following scriptures and write each purpose of fasting:

- **Esther 4:16** _____

- **Jonah 3:5** _____

- **Acts 13:2-3** _____

- **Nehemiah 1:3-4** _____

Just in these four passages, we see fasting for the purposes of preparing to make a major decision, repentance, getting ready to undertake an important work, and for grief.

Read Matthew 6:16. How does Jesus describe the hypocrites when they fast? _____

_____

The hypocrites craved that praise from men so badly! They would walk around with a sad face so that everyone would be sure to know that they were fasting. In this way, they would be praised for their self-denial and their seemingly obvious devotion to God. Jesus says they had the reward they wanted for their fasting, but it had nothing whatsoever to do with devotion to God. Jesus then explains how a person with pure motives in fasting should look in verses 17 and 18. How does he describe that person?_____

_____

_____

No one would know this person was fasting because it would not be outwardly obvious to anyone. It was only between that person and God – as it should be.

The Golden Rule

Read Matthew 7:12. This verse is often referred

to as the Golden Rule and is used as a guide for how we should treat others.

> The Golden Rule is not a reaction to how others treat us but is a proactive way for us to treat others.

Luke 6:31 is the parallel passage to this which is followed by seven verses that deal with our motives for the way we treat others. Let's take a closer look at pure motives in our relationships.

Read Luke 6:32-38. How easy is it to do something nice for someone who always does nice things for you? How easy is it to love someone who loves you? It's very easy and it is a joy. However, how easy is it to love someone who never treats you well? Jesus gets to the heart of the matter where relationships with other people are concerned when he says in Luke 6:32, *"But if you love those who love you, what credit is that to you?"* In other words, why should you get a pat on the back for doing something so obviously easy? Whom does Jesus say does the very same thing at the end of that verse? _____
It's not a challenge to love or to do good to those who love and are good to us. The challenge comes in loving with a pure heart those who do not love us in return.

Jesus says the same thing regarding doing good and lending. Even the sinners will do good to those who do good to them and will lend to those from whom they hope to receive something back. If we are going to be set apart as Christians, we must go beyond what people of the world will do. We must imitate what Christ would do. Jesus Christ loved his enemies, did good to those who despised him and helped those who could never give him anything in return. Why? He had pure motives in his relationships with people. He had true love for each person he came in contact with. He also had the ultimate desire to do all things to please and serve his Father in heaven. **Read John 8:29b** and write it here. _____

_____

Read Luke 6:35-38. Jesus says we are to love our enemies, do good, and lend, hoping for what?_____

_____

Having the right motives in dealing with others will result in reward from our heavenly Father because we will be imitators of Him. How does verse 35 say the Lord treats the unthankful and evil? _____
Because He is so loving and merciful, we are to do no less. What are we commanded to be in verse 36?

_____

_____

If we secretly become upset when someone doesn't return a kindness, then that is in indicator that we didn't do the kindness with the right intent in the first place. Showing mercy to others with pure motives means we will have no expectation of anything in return from them, and we are perfectly okay with that. Our goal should always be to please God and to honor Him by serving someone else.

In verse 37, Jesus addresses three difficult areas: judging, condemnation, and forgiveness. Do we ever find it all too easy to judge others and maybe even delight in condemning them? Why do you think we do that? _____

_____

Could it be because it makes us somehow feel better about ourselves to look down on someone who is "worse than" us? Judging and condemning are definitely symptoms of a Pharisee complex. The Pharisees were a group of Jewish religious leaders who liked to think more highly of themselves than they ought to have. They were self-righteous and had no hesitations about judging and condemning others who were "not as good as" they were. They were definitely not known for their kindness, compassion or mercy. Jesus had some harsh words for them on account of this. **Read Matthew 23:23.** How does Jesus refer to the Pharisees? _____

They were acting out a religious life and pretending to have a faith that only went skin deep but never penetrated to their hearts. Jesus is warning us as well in Luke 6:37 to not be like the Pharisees who judged, condemned and did not forgive. What does Jesus say we will receive if we are willing to forgive others?

Finally, in Luke 6:38, Jesus encourages us to give with the right motives. We are to be generous and sincere in our giving. I once heard a great illustration about giving: If your fist is closed tight, holding on to what you have, it will not be open to receive anything in return. The Lord knows if we are being stingy or selfish in our hearts in regard to our giving and it will be reflected in the way He gives to us. If we give openly and gladly, God will pour out abundant blessings back to us.

Conclusion

If we are to be purer in heart, we must have pure motives in our service to God, in our service to others, and in our relationships with others. Motives matter!

<u>For Thought or Discussion</u>:

1. Think of the example of the woman in the beginning of this lesson. Were her motives for helping the church pure? Why or why not?

2. What is the definition of a hypocrite?

3. What three areas from the Sermon on the Mount were discussed in this lesson in regards to the motives of a hypocrite versus the motives of a righteous person? What motivated the hypocrites?

4. What does the Golden Rule say?

5. What was Jesus' motivation in serving His Father? (John 8:29b)

6. Read Galatians 1:10 and I Thessalonians 2:4-6. What was Paul's motive in preaching the gospel? What did he say he did not use and did not seek?

7. From the discussion of Luke 6:32-38, are there any areas that you struggle with in your relationships with others? What steps can you take toward changing your heart?

Challenge:

Carefully and honestly examine why you do the things you do. Are your works of service and good deeds being done for the glory of men or the glory of God? Are your relationships with others what they ought to be? If you are struggling in one or both of these areas, read the Sermon on the Mount each day, focusing on the scriptures that address the area(s) you need to grow in. Journal your struggles, what changes you are making, and the results.

Prayer Request:

Pray for a heart that has only pure motives in living for God and serving Him. Ask the Lord for help in conquering pride and growing in humility. Ask for help and strength to imitate Jesus in how you deal with people and to look at each person as God sees them.

Commit to Memory:

"And whatever you do, do it heartily, as to the Lord and not to men." ~Colossians 3:23

Lesson 6: Purity In Our Attitudes

One of the first Bible verses my children ever had to memorize was **Philippians 2:14** which says, *"Do all things without murmuring and complaining."* Obedience to parents, teachers, or even God does not count for much when it is done with a bad attitude. God not only wants obedience with the right motives as we studied in our last lesson but with the right attitude as well.

The Example of Israel

God's people, the Israelites, had lived in the land of Egypt as slaves for many years and begged for God's deliverance from their harsh life of bondage. God sent his servant Moses to bring the people out of Egyptian bondage and into the promised land of Canaan. The people saw the mighty miracles which God performed through the 10 plagues He brought upon Egypt: He turned water into blood, sent frogs, lice, and flies in swarms so numerous they infiltrated the houses and covered the people, He struck their cattle and livestock with disease, covered the Egyptians and their animals with painful boils, sent fire and ice from heaven, covered the land with locusts and darkness, and finally He struck the firstborn of all the land of Egypt except for the faithful Hebrews who had the blood of a lamb on their doorposts. And if that were not enough, the Israelites saw the awesomeness of God at work again as He parted the Red Sea, allowing them to cross on dry land, yet drowning Pharaoh's entire army as they pursued them. Time and time again, God's power and might were demonstrated before His people and yet, they didn't believe Him capable of providing for them or protecting them on their journey to the promised land. They murmured and complained, not once, but numerous times. Read the following scriptures and write down what the Israelites were murmuring and complaining about in each instance:

- **Exodus 15:24** _____

  _____

- **Exodus 16:2-3** _____

  _____

- **Exodus 17:3** _____

  _____

- **Numbers 14:2-4** _____

  _____

- **Numbers 16:8-11** _____

_____

- **Numbers 16:41** _____

_____

- **Numbers 21:5** _____

_____

The Israelites complained about their physical needs such as food and water. Why? Was there any reason to doubt that God Almighty who brought the 10 plagues upon Egypt and parted the Red Sea was somehow unable to provide food and water for His people?

They also complained about the promised land of Canaan. They heard the report from 10 of the 12 spies that there were giants in the land and they instantly thought that they had been purposely brought there to be killed. They were so discontented and upset, they actually proposed all-out rebellion against God by wanting to appoint a new leader to take them right back to Egypt. Psalm 106:24-25 says, *"Then they despised the pleasant land; they did not believe His word. But **murmured** in their tents, and did not heed the voice of the Lord."* They would rather have returned to a harsh life of slavery instead of trusting in God to give them what He had already promised.

Some of the Levites complained about the fact

that they weren't priests like Aaron and his sons and it just wasn't fair in their eyes. They wanted to be important like Moses and Aaron apparently were. After all, why shouldn't some of the others get to be leaders too? They complained when God punished and killed the rebels among them. They were actually upset that God's justice had been carried out against those who had boldly been disobedient and rebellious against Him. They didn't seem to think that their sin should carry any consequences.

And finally, they had the audacity to complain about the food God so mercifully provided for them by calling His manna, *"this worthless bread."* How do you think God felt as He listened to complaint after complaint against Him?

How Does God View Murmuring and Complaining?

God had a response to every instance of murmuring and complaining by His people. Read each of the following scriptures and write down God's response:

• **Exodus 15:25-26** _____

_____

• **Exodus 16:4** _____

_____

- **Exodus 17:5-7** _____

  _____

- **Numbers 14:11-12, 20-23** _____

  _____

- **Numbers 16:30-35** _____

  _____

- **Numbers 16:44-49** _____

  _____

- **Numbers 21:6** _____

  _____

Notice that a progression takes place in God's responses to His people's sin of murmuring and complaining. At first, God is merciful and provides the things which they feel are lacking although He does say He is testing them. Testing them how? He wants to see if they will be faithful to Him and walk in His ways. He wants them to have implicit trust in Him and know that He will do exactly what He says He will do. If the Israelites had had the proper attitude, they would have done just that. They would have thanked God and praised Him for His mercy and providential care. Instead they were not thankful for what He provided and refused to trust in Him. As the complaining continued, God's patience and long-suffering reached their limit and punishment occurred. The earth opening up to swallow men alive, fire coming down from heaven to consume, serpents biting the people, and a deadly plague which kills thousands for murmuring and complaining may seem extreme, harsh, and cruel, but they are not. When the Israelites murmured and complained, it was not just a little whining every now and then about what they had to eat or how long the trip was taking. God saw their hearts and what He observed was not pretty and certainly not pure. He saw hearts that were filled with ingratitude, hearts that trusted in themselves and not in God, hard hearts that were stubborn and willful and rebellious, hearts that had no reverence, respect, or love for their Lord. The Israelites should have kept in mind that "grumbling leads to stumbling".³ Their murmuring and complaining led to serious sin on their part followed by severe consequences from the Lord God. They could have stopped all of this in its tracks if they had guarded their hearts against complaining by filling it with thankfulness instead.

An Attitude of Gratitude

How can we guard ourselves against developing the habit of murmuring and complaining? A heart that is discontent and murmurs is one that is ungrateful. Developing an attitude of gratitude is a natural remedy for murmuring and complaining. A thankful person is a contented, happy person. She focuses on what she *does* have rather than what she does *not* have. She chooses to count her blessings rather than make a list of

3   B.J. Clarke

everything that's missing from her life. She chooses to see the glass half-full rather than half-empty and she chooses to see roses on thorns rather than thorns on roses. Did you notice how many times the word "choose" is used? Being thankful is a conscience choice that we must make until it becomes second nature to us. It is also a conscience decision to keep our focus on God rather than our circumstances. When we take our eyes off of God and start looking around us, we can very easily become discontented and the complaining will soon begin. When we take our eyes off of our own circumstances and look to God, our hearts will be overflowing with thankfulness for everything He has done for us and continues to do.

Read each of the following scriptures about thankfulness. Take note of how often we should be thankful, how we are to thank God and what we should thank Him for:

- **Colossians 3:15** _____

  _____

- **Ephesians 5:20** _____

  _____

- **Psalm 100:4** _____

  _____

- **Psalm 106:1** _____

  _____

- **Psalm 118:28-29** _____

_____

An attitude of gratitude consists of praising God for who He is and what He does for us, being thankful always for all things. It is an attitude that dispels discontent from our hearts and prevents murmuring and complaining.

Attitude Toward Others

Not only is purity in our attitude toward God important, but we must also have a pure attitude toward others. This can be difficult, especially when we are faced with dealing with people who make it hard to get along with them. In **Luke 6:32-33**, Jesus challenges us to love others who are unlovable and to do good to those who may not seem deserving of being treated well. He does this by asking some rhetorical questions. He asks, *"But if you love those who love you, what credit is that to you? For even sinners love those who love them. And if you do good to those who do good to you, what credit is that to you? For even sinners do the same."* He knows how easy it is for anyone, sinner or believer, to love someone who loves you and is good to you. That doesn't require any real effort on our part, does it? But it is so much harder to show kindness and to actually love someone who mistreats us, hurts us, or is downright hateful toward us. How do we accomplish this? It is certainly not through our own feelings. We will never automatically feel "warm fuzzies" for people like that. It is through choosing to love others and treating them the way God requires us to. He gives us guidelines for this in Romans 12. Take a few minutes and **read Romans chapter 12**. This chapter is a great reminder of how we should focus our full attention on God, offer ourselves to Him as a living sacrifice, and love and treat others in the way He would have us. In verse 9 we are told, *"Let love be without hypocrisy."* In other words, we are not allowed to fake it! Our love for others must be pure and genuine, just as God's great love is toward us. In verse 14 we are told, *"Bless those who persecute you; bless and do not curse."* God knows that the temptation for us to lash back at others in anger is strong, but He commands us to rise above those feelings. He wants us to utilize the fruits of the Spirit: love, joy, peace, patience, kindness, goodness, faithfulness, gentleness, and self-control (Galatians 5:22-23) and instead of anger and cursing, blessing the one who persecutes and hurts you.

Read Romans 12:17-21. Write verse 21 here.

_____

_____

We can never hope to achieve this through our own human nature. Peter tells us in II Peter 1:3-4 that we need to be partakers of the divine nature, that is, be imitators of God. We need to move beyond what our flesh *wants* to do and reach higher. **Read II Peter 1:3-7.** Peter says we begin with a foundation of faith and then build up from there, adding a brick at a time. Write down, in order, each item we need to add to our faith:

_____

_____

_____

This is not simple nor a quick fix. Peter tells us in verse 5 that we need to *"give all diligence"* to adding these Christian graces to our lives. It will take hard work and effort, but we are promised in I Peter 1:10, *"...for if you do these things you will never stumble."*

Conclusion

In order to be purer in heart, we must be pure in our attitudes both toward God and others. Do not murmur and complain, but develop an attitude of gratitude. Love others without hypocrisy and overcome evil with good.

For Thought or Discussion:

1. Why is purity in our attitudes so important?

2. What were some of the things the Israelites complained about?

3. How does God feel about murmuring and complaining from His people?

4. What is a natural remedy for complaining?

5. Besides the scriptures listed in this lesson, what other verses can you find on the subject of thankfulness?

6. In order to love others as God commands us to, we must rise above human nature (our own feelings) and be "partakers of the divine nature." How do we partake of the divine nature according to II Peter 1:3-7?

7. Read Romans 12 every day for the next week and strive to apply its principles to your daily life.

Challenge:

#1 Do you murmur and complain? Be honest! Maybe you don't do it out loud, but do you find yourself doing it mentally? Are you fostering feelings of discontent in your heart? Make a conscience effort to stop this. Every time you catch yourself feeling unhappy about something, stop and think of five things (or more) that you are thankful for and praise God for them. Develop an attitude of gratitude.

#2 Do you have trouble getting along with certain people or loving them as you know you should? Take the time to pray for them each day. It may not change them, but it can help change your attitude toward them. Read Romans 12 when you need help with this.

Prayer Request:

Praise the Lord and thank Him for who He is and for what He does for you. Ask Him to help you develop a thankful heart and to put away any complaining and murmuring. Ask the Lord for strength, patience, and love in dealing with others in the proper way, a way that is pleasing to Him.

Commit to Memory:

"Do all things without murmuring and complaining." ~Philippians 2:14

Lesson 7: Purity In Our Dress

For many women, fashion is our passion. We may enjoy the latest styles and trends or just like wearing something new and pretty. We don't like to be dressed in something that makes us feel plain or frumpy, but rather, we want to feel beautiful and feminine. There is nothing wrong with wanting to feel feminine and beautiful through the clothes we wear. Even the virtuous woman in Proverbs 31 dressed well. **Read Proverbs 31:22.** How is her clothing described?

_____

However, a serious problem arises if the latest fashions we're wearing happen to be immodest and inappropriate. Are we actively practicing purity in our dress?

Hidden Treasure

Read Isaiah 45:3. Where are riches and treasures found? _____

Boxing champion Muhammad Ali had two daughters and on one occasion when they were grown, they visited their father wearing clothes that were not modest. He taught them about modesty by giving them an object lesson. He told the girls that everything valuable that God made was hidden and hard to get to. For example, where do you find pearls? Tucked within an oyster shell at the bottom of the sea. Where are diamonds found? Deep down in the ground as is gold which has to be uncovered and mined out of the rocks. You have to work hard to obtain these valuable treasures because they are well concealed. He then told his girls that their bodies were valuable, much more so than pearls or diamonds or gold and they should be hidden as well.

Modesty Defined

The word "modesty" has several definitions, but in this lesson we want to focus on its meaning as it relates to the clothes we wear. "Modesty means propriety. It means avoiding clothes and adornment that are extravagant or sexually enticing. Modesty is humility expressed in dress. It's a desire to serve others, particularly men, by not promoting or provoking sensuality. "[4] This definition of modesty has a couple of things we should consider.

First, immodesty can be expressed by extravagance and gaudiness. These types of clothes may not reveal skin or be tight-fitting, but if they are outlandish, bright, or eccentric, it could be considered immodest. You've probably experienced this before if

---

4 C.J. Mahaney, *God, My Heart, and Clothes*, 2.

you have ever seen someone in a restaurant or a store that was wearing something so "over-the-top", outlandish, or ridiculous that everybody stared at them or looked their way as they walked by. Drawing so much attention to oneself could be a clue that you are dressing immodestly. It does not show propriety which means it is not decent, appropriate, or proper.

Second, the above definition shows us that anything that is sexually enticing is immodest. Ladies, we need to keep in mind that males are stimulated and attracted *visually*. That is the way that God created them. **Read II Samuel 11:1-5.** There has been much discussion as to whether Bathsheba was at fault by bathing out in the open or whether she may have been down in a courtyard and the fault was strictly David's for strolling on a rooftop where he had a commanding view of what was below. Whatever the case, what is clear from this text is that Bathsheba was bathing in a position where someone else was able to view her, and the sight of her beautiful body so tempted David that he sent for her and committed adultery with her without any immediate regard for the gravity of that sin. What consequence of that sin do we read in verse 5?_____

_____

The consequences didn't stop there. David desperately wanted to cover up what had happened so no one would know. **Read II Samuel 11:6-25.** What was another result of David's sin with Bathsheba?_____

_____

_____

We see David falling further and further into sin. He resorts to having Bathsheba's husband Uriah murdered and shows no remorse over his crime. **Read II Samuel 11:26-27.** What was the Lord's attitude toward David even after David married Bathsheba? _____

_____

David's sin didn't stop with the act of adultery and as you read through the book of II Samuel, you will see that the consequences of these sins had far-reaching effects for David and his family. Where did it all begin? With a godly man seeing the beautiful body of a woman that did not belong to him.

We have a serious responsibility to not make it hard on the opposite sex by wearing enticing clothing. What do I mean by enticing? Showing too much skin, plunging necklines that reveal cleavage, short skirts or shorts, tight-fitting pants and tops that outline curves, clingy dresses, see-through material, bare midriffs – all of these things are designed to be "sexy" and enticing. It makes men both young and old want to look and the looking leads to thinking – thinking thoughts they should not. Some women will try to defend themselves and the way they dress by accusing men who think such things as "having a dirty mind." These women and girls refuse to take any responsibility for their part in the men's thoughts. It is true that there will be some men who would look at a woman and lust after her in their heart even if she were dressed in a burlap bag. However, these men already have a sin problem. There are plenty of good Christian men who are trying to avoid sinful thoughts, but we might be making it very hard for them if we're putting our bodies on display in immodest clothing.

I once read about a hijacking that took place on a luxury yacht by some pirates a few decades ago. There were several men and women on this cruise and many of the women were up on the deck in bathing suits, shorts, etc. when they saw the boatload of pirates approaching. What do you think these women did? They booked it down to their cabins as fast as they could and dressed in clothes that covered them from head to toe, hoping it would help avoid any bodily assault from taking place. They didn't want to entice these men in any way to think provocative thoughts by dressing immodestly in front of them. The point is, if we are honest with ourselves, we girls know full well what is modest, what is not, and what effect our clothing (or lack thereof) has on men.

What to Wear?

Keeping up with the latest fashions is only okay insofar as they are modest fashions that please God and are harmless to the men we come in contact with, especially our Christian brothers. Just because miniskirts, low necklines, or skinny jeans may be what "everybody" is wearing, it doesn't make it right and acceptable. We need to be very mindful of this each day as we make our clothing selections. Does this mean that we may not always "fit in" with what other people wear? Probably. **Read II Corinthians 6:17a** and write it on the lines. _____

_____

_____

The Lord has never expected or desired His people to be like everybody else, but on the contrary, He wants us to be distinctly different. Our first love is the Lord and our desire to please and serve Him should come before everything else.

> Dressing modestly is something the Lord desires and requires of His daughters.

So, what is the well-dressed Christian woman wearing these days? **Read I Timothy 2:9-10**. What three things are women to adorn themselves with?

_____

_____

Paul says women shouldn't be adorning themselves with braided hair, gold, pearls, or expensive clothing.

Does this mean that it's a sin to braid your hair? No. He is not prohibiting, but making a point about where a godly woman's focus ought to be: on modest dress, a humble spirit, and a doer of good works rather than focusing on dressing like a peacock to impress the masses. Following the latest trends in clothing, hairstyles and jewelry is nothing new to us today. During the time that Paul was writing this, it was common for women to experiment with elaborate hairstyles consisting of braids with strands of gold and pearls intricately interwoven and wound about the head. Expensive clothing was easily recognizable and meant to impress others with your wealth and social status. Only worldly women would be concerned with such things; godly women would not. This is exactly what Paul is explaining. Peter echoed some similar thoughts. **Read I Peter 3:3-4.** He also tells the women not to be focused on the hairstyles, jewelry, and clothing, but to dress themselves with an ornament that is very precious to God. What ornament is it? ____

_____

Read Proverbs 31:30 and write it here.

_____

_____

_____

A godly woman isn't obsessed with and focused on outward beauty, but has a heart rightly focused on God. **Read I Peter 5:5-6.** What else is a godly woman to be clothed with? _____

Read Deuteronomy 22:5. What is a godly woman **not** to be clothed with? _____

_____

We need to consider this admonition very carefully. There is a strong description of this behavior in this verse. The Lord considers it an abomination. An abomination is something disgusting, loathsome, and absolutely intolerable to God.

> There are many things that have become acceptable in our society to the point that even Christians may not be bothered too much by them, but if something is an abomination to God, we must share that same conviction and not think a certain behavior is okay simply because it is socially acceptable.

"Cross-dressing" isn't funny, acceptable, or no big deal. It is wrong! Women wearing men's clothing is wrong and we need to take that seriously. God created men to be men and women to be women and we are to fill the role God gave us in every way, including dressing in a feminine manner.

The Well-dressed Godly Woman

Let's revisit the well-dressed virtuous woman of Proverbs 31. **Read Proverbs 31:25a** to see what else a godly women clothes herself with and write it here:

_____

_____

_____

From the scriptures we have studied in this lesson, we should have no trouble deciding what we are to wear. We have seen what the modest, well-dressed Christian lady and young lady wears:

- *Modest apparel, propriety and moderation (I Timothy 2:9,10)*

- *A gentle and quiet spirit (I Peter 3:3,4)*

- *Clothes that pertain to a woman (Deuteronomy 22:5)*

- *Strength and honor (Proverbs 31:25a)*

The bottom line concerning modesty in our dress is that God requires His daughters to be women of modesty both in our hearts and in our outward appearance. In serving our Father the King, we dress each day in a pure way that will always be pleasing to Him.

Conclusion

Are there clothes in your closet that do not

represent a pure heart? In order to be purer in heart, we must give serious consideration to the way we dress so that it is truly modest, humble, and God-honoring.

For Thought or Discussion:

1. In the given definition of modesty, one sentence reads, "*Modesty is humility expressed in dress.*" How does dressing modestly show humility?

2. Why is humility an important characteristic of a Christian woman?

3. How does dressing modestly serve others?

4. In I Timothy 2:9-10, what are some of the outward manifestations of beauty that women can focus too much on?

5. In I Peter 3:5, what kind of women adorned themselves with a *"gentle and quiet spirit"*?

6. Does reading Deuteronomy 22:5 make you reconsider any items of your clothing? Why or why not?

7. How can you clothe yourself with strength and honor?

Challenge:

Look through all of the clothes, shoes, and accessories you own. Honestly assess everything and if there is anything which you know is immodest and not God-honoring, get rid of it. A good mantra to follow: "When in doubt, throw it out!"

Prayer Request:

Ask the Lord for an open and honest heart as you assess your wardrobe. Ask Him for strength and wisdom to make right decisions as to what you wear and how you present yourself before others.

Commit to Memory:

"In like manner also, that the women adorn themselves in modest apparel, with propriety and moderation, not with braided hair or gold or pearls or costly clothing, but, which is proper for women professing godliness, with good works." ~I Timothy 2:9,10

Lesson 8: Purity In Our Bodies

"For You have formed my inward parts; You have covered me in my mother's womb. I will praise You, for I am fearfully and wonderfully made; marvelous are Your works, and that my soul knows very well. My frame was not hidden from You, when I was made in secret, and skillfully wrought in the lowest parts of the earth." ~Psalm 139:13-15

David pens a beautiful description in this passage of how God formed him in his mother's womb. We, like David, were lovingly and carefully crafted by our heavenly Father. He knew each of us before we were born, before we were even conceived, and He has seen all the days of our lives before they ever began. (Psalms 139:16) He knows each one of us so intimately that Matthew 10:30 tells, *"But the very hairs of your head are all numbered."*

To Whom Do Our Bodies Belong?

Read I Corinthians 3:16-17. The apostle Paul compares our bodies to a temple. This temple does not stand empty but is used as a dwelling place by the Holy Spirit. In view of that fact, how should we present our temples? _____

_____

Do we want them to be filthy, littered with trash, unholy, and uninviting? Or do we want them to be clean, pure, holy and open for the indwelling of the Holy Spirit? The condition of our temples will depend upon the purity of our bodies.

How many times have you heard these kinds of statements in today's culture: "I can do what I want because it's my body." "It's my choice because it's my body." We hear statements such as these quite frequently as a defense of many sins. If someone wants to justify something they do with their body such as adultery, fornication, homosexuality, or even abortion, the claim is made that their body belongs to themselves, therefore, they have a right to do whatever they want with it or to it. Is this a valid defense? **Read I Corinthians 6:19-20**. Whom does Paul say that our bodies belong to?_____
If we believe the words of the Bible, and understand that our bodies do *not* belong to us but to God, how will that govern our behavior and the choices that we make which involve our bodies? _____

_____

_____

_____

Sexual Immorality

When we think about purity in connection with our physical bodies, we usually associate it with sexual purity. While there are other sins that are connected with our bodies, sexual sins are certainly very important to address, specifically because the Bible has quite a lot to say about them.

Read I Corinthians 6:13-18. What does Paul say the body is not for? _____
What is the body for? _____
Sexual immorality is the one sin that the Bible says is against our own body. Sexual immorality is also referred to as fornication. This includes any sex outside of a marriage relationship including pre-marital sex, adultery, homosexuality, incest, prostitution, and any type of sexual perversion. How does verse 18 say we should avoid sexual immorality? _____
_____

In the book of Genesis, we can read the account of a young man who literally ran to avoid fornication. **Read Genesis 39:1-12.** Think about the situation that Joseph found himself in – he was all alone in the house with a married woman who was trying to seduce him. If he gave in, who would know? Certainly not Potiphar (the woman's husband) nor any of the servants. What reason did Joseph give for not committing such a sin in verse 9? _____
Joseph would naturally have been concerned about

abusing the trust of his employer, but that was not the reason he abstained from fornication. Joseph did not want to commit such wickedness before God and was so strong in his resolve that he tore himself away from the grasp of Potiphar's wife and ran out of the house, leaving his garment in her hand. The Lord takes sexual immorality that seriously. We are to flee it at all costs.

Read I Thessalonians 4:3-8. God has sanctified us, setting us apart for holy living and for His glory. Any kind of sexual immorality is incompatible with a life of purity and holiness. What does God call us to?

_____

What are we not called to? _____

Read each of the following verses concerning sexual immorality:

- **Ephesians 5:3, 5**

- **Hebrews 13:4**

- **I Corinthians 6:9-10**

- **Galatians 5:19-21**

What will the sexually immoral not inherit?

_____

What should the marriage bed be? _____

A marriage bed is to be pure when a husband and wife come together in it, not corrupted with any kind of sexual immorality. Many married couples have experienced difficulties in their sex life because of past or present sexual sins. When the marriage bed is defiled, serious problems arise as a result. Sexual sin is ultimately so serious because one will be judged by God and condemned because of it. The Lord is clear that fornicators have no inheritance in the kingdom of God. If you have been guilty of any type of sexual immorality, please do not think it is too late for you to have a life of purity. It is never too late because our God is a God of forgiveness and hope! This will be addressed further in a later lesson.

If you are single at this time, please don't think that "technical virginity" is okay. That is, thinking it's okay to allow certain things to happen in a physical relationship with someone as long as you don't "go all the way." Let's consider the point that allowing some physical intimacy isn't really harmful. Take a big, beautiful, juicy apple and take a large bite out of it then set it aside for several hours. Now, place that apple (bite side up) in a basket of other apples which have been untouched. If you offer the basket of apples to others, which apples will they choose? Which apple will most likely not be chosen and why? The apple with the bite out of it has part of it missing and there is a brown, stained spot left behind. It is less desirable than the apples which are whole and unstained. When you allow *any* physical intimacies with a man, you are giving away part of yourself, including a part of your heart. Save all of your heart and your body for the one person you will pledge to love for the rest of your life.

You will be so glad that you did.

Other Sins Involving Our Bodies

Besides any kind of sexual sin, there are other sins which can defile our temples, making them impure. Let's briefly examine two:

- Drunkenness

- Gluttony

I believe we all understand what drunkenness is, but we might not really have a grasp on the definition of gluttony or why it is condemned in the Bible. What exactly is gluttony? Webster's dictionary defines it as "excess in eating; extravagant indulgence of the appetite for food." What about having second helpings? Is that wrong? There is nothing wrong with food in and of itself or enjoying good food. Gluttony is sinful because it is an unrestrained indulgence of food. Someone who gorges themselves on food is not only harming their body physically, but they are also demonstrating a lack of self-control.

Our appetites should not define and control us, but rather, we should control our appetites.

Solomon so candidly puts it this way in **Proverbs 23:2,** *"Put a knife to your throat if you are a man given to appetite."*

Read the following scriptures and briefly note what they say about the two sins of drunkenness and gluttony which often go hand-in-hand:

- **Ephesians 5:18** _____

_____

- **Proverbs 20:1** _____

_____

- **Proverbs 23:29-32** _____

_____

- **Philippians 3:19** _____

_____

- **Proverbs 25:16** _____

_____

- **Proverbs 23:21** _____

_____

The bottom line can be found in **I Corinthians 10:31** which says, *"Therefore, whatever you eat or drink, or whatever you do, do all to the glory of God."* Is what we are eating or drinking, or how we are eating and drinking glorifying to God or in defiance of His Word?

105

Cleansing the Temple

In both the Old and New Testaments, the temple in Jerusalem was looked upon and referred to as the house of God. It was the place of holiness where God's people came to meet Him through their worship and sacrifices to Him. Many times through the centuries, that temple became corrupted as it was filled with idols, false worship and in Jesus' day, thieves. On more than one occasion, a righteous king rose up and cleansed the temple from all filthiness and impurity, making it holy and acceptable once again for the Lord.

Jesus himself was faced with this task and properly rose to the occasion. **Read John 2:13-17.** When Jesus reached Jerusalem for the Passover feast, he found something extremely disturbing taking place in the temple. The courtyard had been turned into a marketplace where the selling of livestock and birds for sacrifices was taking place. The moneychangers had also set up shop and were doing a booming business as well.

The coinage of the Gentiles was commonly in circulation at that time, but it was not accepted at the temple where the Jewish shekel and half-shekel were required to use for offerings. The moneychangers would exchange the Gentile coins for the Jewish shekels at a high rate of exchange thereby making a nice profit for themselves. What they were actually doing was robbing the Jewish people through gouging them financially. How did Jesus react to all of this taking place at his Father's temple? _____

_____

_____

He didn't calmly assess the situation and then politely ask everyone to leave since what they were doing was not appropriate at the Lord's temple. No! He felt righteous indignation at what he witnessed. He fashioned a whip and drove them out of the temple. He overturned the tables of the moneychangers and commanded those who were selling the birds and animals to take them away at once. He used force and took swift action to clean up that temple. He wanted it physically and spiritually cleansed and he wasted no time in doing it. He took drastic steps and was firm in his resolve.

When we acknowledge that there is impurity in our temples that needs to be purged, we should look to the example of Jesus. We don't need to play around with sin and clean up our lives piece-meal and casually. We need to get serious about sin and be willing to take every necessary step to get rid of it. This will sometimes mean that we need to take some drastic action and make some forceful decisions. **Read Colossians 3:5.** What phrase in this verse indicates the forcefulness we should use when getting rid of sin? ___

_____

Any type of sexual sin will lead to nothing short of our soul's condemnation. It is never worth it. If there is any type of sexual sin in your life today, I plead with you to stop, repent, and take every measure necessary to cleanse your temple.

A Living Sacrifice

Read Romans 12:1 and write it here. _____

_____

_____

_____

_____

Notice that we are to present our bodies to God each and every day, and they are to be found holy and acceptable to Him. We do this by not conforming to the world around us, thereby allowing our bodies to become impure as they are touched by worldliness. Paul states it this way in II Corinthians 7:1, *"...let us cleanse ourselves from all filthiness of the flesh and spirit, perfecting holiness in the fear of God."*

Read Romans 6:12-13. What does Paul say we should not let the members of our body be used for?

_____

What *should* all the parts of our body be used for?

_____

Just as God fashioned every part of us from the hair on our head down to the toes on our feet, we must make sure that every part of us is glorifying Him daily.

- Her HAIR is given to her for a covering. (I Corinthians 11:15b)

- Her EYES are ever looking for the glorious appearing of Jesus Christ. (Titus 2:13)

- Her EARS are swift to hear. (James 1:19)

- Her MOUTH opens with wisdom, and her TONGUE has the law of kindness on it. (Proverbs 31:26)

- Her HEART rejoices in the Lord. (I Samuel 2:1)

- Her BODY is clothed with strength and honor. (Proverbs 31:25)

- Her HANDS work willingly. (Proverbs 31:13b)

- Her FEET walk in love. (Ephesians 5:2)

Conclusion

A woman dedicated to God brings God glory through every part of her. She doesn't pretend to have a pure heart while dishonoring God by what she looks at with her eyes, hears with her ears, says with her mouth, or touches with her hands. She understands that her body belongs to the One who lovingly and tenderly created her and she uses it for His glory. Being pure in our bodies is a huge and necessary step in becoming purer in heart.

For Thought or Discussion:

1. As you read Psalm 139:13-15, how does it make you feel that God lovingly created you and knows you so intimately?

2. Besides sexual sins, drunkenness and gluttony, what else can you think of that defiles us or is harmful to our bodies?

3. What reason did Joseph give for not committing fornication and how did he avoid it?

4. Why was Jesus so angry over the condition of the temple?

5. What Old Testament examples can you find of kings cleansing the temple in Jerusalem?

6. Romans 12:1 says our bodies should be a living sacrifice. What exactly does that mean?

7. In what ways can our bodies glorify God?

Challenge:

This challenge can be a tough one. Take a long, honest look at your life and decide if everything you do with your body is glorifying to God. If you have a problem with gluttony, challenge yourself to conquer this sin. If you are struggling with any type of sexual sin, repent of it and resolve to stay strong in the Lord by maintaining a pure body. Cleanse your temple and make it a welcome, holy home for God's Holy Spirit.

Prayer Request:

Ask the Lord for the strength needed to conquer any sins that are defiling your body. Ask Him to put faithful Christian sisters in your life to help you stay accountable if that's what it takes to overcome any sin you're struggling with.

Commit to Memory:

"I beseech you therefore, brethren, by the mercies of God, that you present your bodies a living sacrifice, holy, acceptable to God, which is your reasonable service."

~Romans 12:1

Lesson 9: Purity In Our Religion

There was once a woman who was dating a man which attended the same church as she did. This man was a widower, a nice man, faithful in church attendance, and kind and gentle. This man and woman started going out to lunch, then dinner, eventually spending more and more time together. The woman really liked this man and felt safe with him as a good Christian man so she didn't worry about anything getting out of hand. Before long, however, his behavior toward her began to change. He began to make her uncomfortable and eventually she was astonished and offended at his physically inappropriate behavior. When he asked her what was the matter, she responded that she was shocked that a Christian man like him would act in such a manner. He simply smiled at her and said, "Honey, I'm not *that* religious!"

Hypocrisy

Many people in the world today are turned off by the church and Christianity because they see the hypocrisy in the lives of so many Christians like the man above. Too many times in the lives of Christians we're just "not that religious." We're content to attend church and go through the motions, but to actually let Christianity permeate every area of our lives? No way!

This is compartmentalizing our religion. In other words, God and church are for Sunday only, but the rest of the week, I have my work, my recreation, my hobbies, my friends and family, etc., and God and the church don't fit in those areas! This dangerous mentality is why we need to work at purity in our religion, so that the Lord *does* exist and reign in every area of our lives – not just on Sundays when we're at the church building.

> *"They had been instructed theoretically in their religion, but never required to bring it into daily practice."*

This quote from the novel *Mansfield Park* by Jane Austen sadly illustrates how one may "have" religion but it doesn't take root and show its effects in daily life. Let's see how the Bible defines pure religion.

Read James 1:27 and write it here. _____

_____

_____

James identifies the two areas of pure religion: 1) Visiting the widows and orphans, and 2) Keeping oneself unspotted from the world.

What does it mean to visit the orphans and widows? It is not simply a "dropping by to say hi" type of visit. It is visiting them *"in their affliction"*. These are people who sincerely have a need and our job is to go and try to fill that need in whatever way that we can. It is an active service, not a lip service. James addresses the lip service problem in the next chapter, chapter 2, in his discussion of faith vs. works. **Read James 2:14-17.** What are many tempted to do when they see someone who has a need? _____

_____

_____

They are basically saying, "God bless you! Hope things get better for you!" What good has that done the individual? None! If we are practicing a true, pure religion, then our natural desire will be one of service. We will not only respond to needs as we see them, but we will even actively seek out opportunities to help others with whatever resources we have. As lovers of God, we will eagerly desire to serve Him through our service to others.

Sometimes we are confused as to whom we should actually help and in what ways. It is a sad truth that there are people in the world who actively try to take advantage of others, especially the compassionate

Christians. We want to be good stewards of the resources God has blessed us with so it is important to be *"wise as serpents and harmless as* doves*"* as Jesus advises in Matthew 10:16. **Read I Timothy 5:3-16** for some good guidelines as to the care and assistance of widows.

The Lord has always had a tender spot in His heart for the fatherless and the widows. Even under the Mosaic law, the Israelites were commanded to be generous and kind to those who were poor and in need. Read the following verses which gave instructions to God's people as to the treatment and help they were to give orphans, widows, and the poor:

- **Exodus 22:22**
- **Deuteronomy 10:18**
- **Deuteronomy 14:29**
- **Deuteronomy 24:19-21**
- **Deuteronomy 26:13**
- **Deuteronomy 27:19**
- **Psalm 146:9**
- **Isaiah 1:17**
- **Jeremiah 22:3**
- **Zechariah 7:10**

List some of the ways God instructed the widows and orphans to be treated in the previous verses: _____

_____

_____

_____

_____

_____

Keeping Unspotted

Visiting the fatherless and the widows in their time of need is only part of the equation of practicing pure religion; the other part is to keep unblemished or unspotted from the world. This sometimes seems like an impossible task as we are bombarded from all sides with worldliness and evil, but we do have the means to keep ourselves untainted. Try this little hands-on experiment to demonstrate what I'm talking about. Fill a shallow pie plate about half full of water. Generously sprinkle pepper all over the surface of the water. The pepper represents the blackness of sin. Place a drop or two of dish detergent on the tip of your finger. The dish detergent represents the cleansing power of Jesus' blood. Stick the tip of that finger in the middle of the pepper-covered water. What do the pepper flakes immediately do? When we are covered with the cleansing power of Jesus' blood, then the darkness of sin is removed far from us. (I John 1:6-7)

This doesn't mean, however, that staying pure amidst the sin is easy. Let's look at two biblical examples who worked at remaining unspotted from the sinful world around them: Lot and Noah.

Lot was the nephew of Abraham who settled in the city of Sodom with his wife and two daughters. The sins of Sodom and its sister city, Gomorrah, were so wicked that God destroyed them with fire and brimstone from heaven. **Read Genesis 19:1-24.** Before the destruction occurred, the Lord mercifully sent two angels to warn Lot to take his family and leave the city in order to be saved from the coming destruction. Lot obeyed and left with his wife and two daughters.

Read II Peter 2:8. How is Lot described while he lived among the wicked in the city of Sodom? _____

_____

_____

He did not go along with the wicked deeds of his fellow citizens nor did he condone their practices, but he spoke out against what he saw and heard and kept himself righteous before God. Difficult, yes, but doable.

Consider Noah and his family as they were building the ark over a period of 120 years. In a previous lesson we've read how the thoughts of the people of that era were evil continually. Noah and his family were, like Lot, surrounded on a daily basis with wickedness. In fact, if anyone's kids could truly say, "Everybody's doing it!", it would be Noah's sons, but

Genesis 6:8 says that, *"Noah found grace in the eyes of the Lord."* Neither Noah nor his family gave in to the ways of those around them. They kept themselves unspotted from the world in which they lived.

If others could do it, we too can keep ourselves unspotted from the world we live in. Read and write the following scriptures that encourage us in this pursuit:

- **Romans 12:9** _____

  _____

- **Matthew 6:33** _____

  _____

  _____

- **Romans 12:2** _____

  _____

  _____

- **II Corinthians 6:14** _____

  _____

  _____

- **II Corinthians 6:17** _____

  _____

  _____

  _____

Put a Muzzle On It!

James encapsulates what pure religion is in chapter 1 verse 27, but if we back up to verse 26, we read of another factor which can affect the purity of our religion. **Read James 1:26** and write it on the lines. _____

_____

_____

_____

James said that there were Christians who thought they were pretty religious, yet they failed to control their tongues. We studied in a previous lesson how important it is to have pure speech; first, because our words always need to be acceptable to God and we will be judged by them, and second, our words are a reflection of what is in our hearts. James says any Christian who doesn't bridle or control his tongue has deceived himself and has a useless religion. Basically, such a Christian is a hypocrite in his heart and it is reflected in his words. This person may think his religion is pure when in reality, it has been rendered absolutely useless.

We learned previously from the passage of James 3:1-12 how hard it is to control our tongues. What's the solution then? King David had a wonderful way with words as we read over and over in the Psalms, and he offers a unique solution to the problem of controlling one's tongue. **Read Psalm 39:1** and write it on the lines. _____

_____

_____

_____

This may seem a little extreme, but David is simply trying to emphasize how important it is to keep control of our tongues and not sin with our words. He paints for us a word picture of muzzling one's own mouth in order to prevent saying something which should not be said. Here again is why scripture memorization is so important. If any of us are struggling with controlling our tongues and it is jeopardizing the purity of our religion, this would be a helpful verse to memorize and repeat to ourselves often.

Conclusion

Purity in our religion is so necessary in order to be an effective light to the world around us, to worship our God in spirit and truth, and to let Him reign over every area of our lives. Commit to being purer in heart by demonstrating true, pure religion.

For Thought or Discussion:

1. In what ways do we compartmentalize our religion?

2. What are some practical ways to "visit" the widows and orphans?

3. According to I Timothy 5:3-16, what is the order of responsibility for the care of widows?

4. Why do you think the Lord gave the Israelites so many scriptures with instructions concerning their treatment and assistance to widows, orphans, and the poor?

5. What are the challenges you face in keeping unspotted from the world around you?

6. Which particular scriptures serve as an encouragement to you in this area?

7. Besides Lot and Noah, what other Bible characters can you think of that worked hard to remain pure and righteous as they lived among the ungodly?

8. In what ways does a lack of controlling our tongue make our religion useless?

Challenge:

Put your religion to the test. Practice pure and undefiled religion by actively seeking to help a widow or orphan with a need in their lives. How can you impact their life directly with your own time and resources?

Prayer Request:

Ask the Lord to help you remain unspotted from the evils of the world around you. Enlist His strength to overcome temptations and ask for His cleansing to keep the blackness of sin far from you. Desire opportunities from Him to be a shining light to a dark world.

Commit to Memory:

"Pure and undefiled religion before God and the Father is this: to visit orphans and widows in their trouble, and to keep oneself unspotted from the world." ~James 1:27

Lesson 10: Purity In Our Lives

"A good tree cannot bear bad fruit, nor can a bad tree bear good fruit. Every tree that does not bear good fruit is cut down and thrown into the fire. Therefore, by their fruits you will know them." ~Matthew 7:18-20

Usually, it takes a while to really get to know someone. If a person is not genuine, she can put on a good show and present a good face to the world for a while, but after a time, her true colors will start to show. On the other hand, if a woman is the "real deal" and truly pure in heart, it will show itself in all of her actions and words, even though she may not realize she is being observed. Consider the example of a woman named Molly...

"A Pure Woman"

Molly is a woman who is "the real deal." She has many good qualities that you can't help but notice if you are around her for any length of time. I would describe Molly as being gentle, kind, gracious, helpful, compassionate, and unselfish. She never seems to tire of helping others and serving in any way that she can.

She always appears to be patient and loving in every circumstance. She is not easily shaken or moved as she clings to a strong faith that is founded on the rock of the Lord Jesus Christ. That faith was her lifeline as her husband of many, many years slowly died of cancer. Molly faithfully cared for her husband at home for as long as she could until it was necessary to call in Hospice care. One of the sisters in our congregation works for Hospice and visited several times with Molly and her husband. After her visit one day, she spoke with one of the Hospice nurses who was caring for Molly's husband. This nurse had been able to observe Molly for a few days and he was impressed with the kind of woman she was. He told my friend from church that Molly was a unique and impressive woman. The words he used to describe her were, "She is a pure woman." Molly passed a test she didn't even know she was taking. Her purity was shining like the sun to others around her who did not even know her. She was demonstrating the life of a Christian woman dedicated to God through her example before others. That nurse was rightly able to identify her as pure by observing the good fruit Molly was producing in her life. What a great example of letting your light shine!

Let's contrast Molly's example with a different kind of woman. **Read Proverbs 11:22.** This verse paints quite a word picture, doesn't it? Can't you just see in your mind's eye a big, fat pig covered in mud with slop dripping from its mouth and a beautiful gold ring

126

attached to its filthy snout? Not a pretty sight! What does Solomon compare that pig to? _____

_____

_____

The gold ring may be lovely in and of itself, but when it is put in the snout of a pig, you don't see the loveliness of the ring – you see the filthiness of the pig. So it is with a young lady or woman who may appear quite beautiful but has given up all modesty and good behavior, choosing rather to wallow in the filth of impurity and sin. You no longer see her beauty because of the filthiness she surrounds herself with and covers herself in.

Read Proverbs 30:12. This is a perfect description of the pig with the gold ring. How many women (Christians included!) think they are pretty good while ignoring the sin in their lives? We all have a choice to make - the filthy pig with a gold ring in its snout or a pure woman, letting her light shine.

Coming Clean

If you've ever seen the original *Charlotte's Web* movie, you might remember the scene where the family was preparing to go to the state fair. Their famous pig, Wilbur, was to be taken for showing and judging to see if he would win a prize. Before they loaded him up in his crate, the farmer's wife went out and gave Wilbur a bath – with buttermilk. She could see how filthy the pig was and she wanted him washed and clean so he would look his best and be presentable before the judge at the fair.

We too will stand before a Judge one day and it won't be a ribbon that's at stake; it will be the destination of our immortal souls. With that in mind, how do we go about cleansing our lives so that the filthiness of sin is washed away and we sparkle with purity? Read the following scriptures and briefly note what we are to do to cleanse and purify ourselves:

- **II Corinthians 7:1** _____

  _____

- **James 4:8** _____

  _____

- **I Peter 1:22** _____

  _____

- **Isaiah 1:16** _____

  _____

- **Psalm 119:9** _____

  _____

To be cleansed of sin and impurity amounts to obedience to God and His commands through faith. As Christians, that entails repentance of sin by ceasing to do what is wrong, having a mind that is focused squarely on the Lord, and a heart that draws nears to

128

Him and delights in obeying His Word. It is believing that the blood of Christ can continually cleanse us from all unrighteousness when we ask for forgiveness.

God is aware when we are making efforts to live lives of purity and it is pleasing to Him. **Read Psalm 18:20-21.** What does the Psalmist say the Lord did for him because he was living righteously?_____

_____

_____

A Holy Life

Living a life of purity is something we should do because God commands it, but He also gives us the why behind the command. **Read I Thessalonians 4:7.** What has God called us to? _____

_____

Read I Peter 1:15-16. Why are we to be holy?

_____

God calls us to a life of holiness. Not moments of holiness, or "when I feel like it" holiness but a complete, all-encompassing life of holiness.

When we think of holiness, we may consider it to be cleanness, moral living, or righteousness and while all of these are certainly characteristic of a holy life, there is even more involved. Living a life of holiness requires us to be separate and set apart.

1. **We separate ourselves from the world.** II Corinthians 6:17a states, *"Therefore, 'Come out from among them and be separate, says the Lord.'"* We live in this world, but we are not to be of the world, being drawn into becoming like those around us. Romans 12:2 warns against this as it states, *"Do not be conformed to this world..."*, and Colossians 3:2 reminds us to, *"Set your mind on things above, not on things on the earth."* Being separate from the world means shunning every thing that is offensive to God and embracing every thing that is God-honoring and righteous. We shouldn't be longingly gazing at everything the world offers that would lead us farther and farther away from our heavenly Father.

In Genesis 19, we read about righteous Lot and his family living in the sinful city of Sodom. God mercifully sent two angels to warn them of the coming destruction and to give them a chance of escape. However, Lot and his family were told by the angels not to look back as they were escaping, no matter what. As Lot, his wife and two daughters reached the safety of the plain city of Zoar, the Lord began to rain down fire and brimstone on Sodom and Gomorrah. Lot and his family had safely separated themselves from the sinful cities slated for destruction, but despite the warning from the angels, Lot's wife chose to look back. As she did so, she was turned to a pillar of salt. Why did she look back? Perhaps it was just a natural curiosity to see what was taking place, but her husband and daughters heard the same destruction and obeyed the Lord by not looking. Perhaps the real reason was that she longed to look back at what she had left behind. Her heart may not have been inclined to escaping a sinful city but yearning for her life to remain as it had been, comfortably living among the heathens and feeling no urgent need to separate herself from them. How tragic for her and how tragic for us if we are enticed by the world and do not see the need or have the desire to separate ourselves from it.

2. **We are set apart for God.** I Peter 2:9 tells us, *"But you are a chosen generation, a royal priesthood, a holy nation, His own special people, that you may proclaim the praises of Him who called you out of darkness into His marvelous light."* Notice what God has called us out of – darkness. This is where separating ourselves from the world comes in. We have to come out of the darkness of this world first in order to be set apart for

God. Setting ourselves apart then requires walking in the light, living a life of purity and holiness, never to return to the darkness. I John 1:6-7 reminds us, *"If we say that we have fellowship with Him, and walk in darkness, we lie and do not practice the truth. But if we walk in the light as He is in the light, we have fellowship with one another, and the blood of Jesus Christ His Son cleanses us from all sin."*

In II Timothy 2:20-22, the apostle Paul describes different vessels in a great house. Some vessels were made of gold or silver and some were made out of clay or wood. Some were vessels of honor and some were vessels of dishonor. We too are vessels. Which kind will we be? Paul encourages us to cleanse ourselves so that we may be sanctified or set apart. At that point, we are a vessel of honor and are useful to our Master. **Read II Timothy 2:20-22.** What advice does Paul give in verse 22? _____

_____

_____

Read Titus 2:5. What characteristics does God expect His daughters to possess? _____

_____

_____

All of these qualities are things that are evident to other people around us. They are characteristics of a pure, holy life and they can have a powerful influence over others. **Read I Peter 3:1.** What does Peter say the pure conduct of a wife may be able to do? _____

_____

_____

_____

The apostle Paul also realized the importance of this spiritual influence as he penned the first half of II Corinthians 6. **Read II Corinthians 6:3-6.** Paul knew that if his behavior caused offense to others, they would not be willing to listen to his preaching of the gospel. He determined, along with his co-workers, to live blameless, pure lives before others to further the spread of the gospel and to be pleasing to God. In what ways did these ministers for God present themselves to the people around them? _____

_____

_____

_____

Conclusion

We are all observed by others and judged by the fruits we bear in our lives. Even children are not immune from this as it states in Proverbs 20:11, *"Even a child is known by his deeds, by whether what he does is pure and right."* In light of that, we need to take seriously the necessity of living a pure, holy life before God and others, to be separate from the darkness of this world and set apart for God's glory.

For Thought or Discussion:

1. What kind of fruit are you bearing in your life?

2. If someone met you for the first time and was around you constantly for one week, how do you think they would honestly describe you?

3. Why do so many people (including some Christians) consider themselves "pure in their own eyes"?

4. What are some ways the Bible teaches of cleansing ourselves?

5. What constitutes holy living?

6. How do we separate ourselves from the world we live in? Do we ever find it difficult to do this and if so, why?

7. How should we conduct ourselves before others in order to demonstrate purity in our lives?

Challenge:

#1 Honestly assess how others around you perceive you. If they couldn't describe you as a pure woman, prune your tree of any bad fruit and begin working to produce beautiful fruit in your life. Pruning can be painful, but it is productive. Read Galatians 5:22-23 and write it or print it out, placing it where you can read it each day to remind you of the kind of fruit you need to bear in your life.

#2 Examine yourself to see if you have been pure in your own eyes while not acknowledging sin in your life. If necessary, cleanse your life of anything that would keep you from standing pure before the Lord, the righteous Judge.

Prayer Request:

Ask the Lord for strength and persistence in producing good fruit. Pray for a heart that desires the righteous things in life and shuns the filth of this world. Pray for the desire to be a good example and influence to those you come in contact with, whether you are aware of the impact you make or not.

Commit to Memory:

"That you may become blameless and harmless, children of God without fault in the midst of a crooked and perverse generation, among whom you shine as lights in the world." ~Philippians 2:15

Lesson 11: Purity – Outward vs. Inward

In our last lesson, we examined the importance of living a life of purity before others so that they may see Christ living in us. Living a pure life on the outside starts with a pure heart on the inside.

When I was teaching a Keepers at Home girls' club at our church, there were many meetings where we worked in the kitchen on some type of cooking or baking project. Before we began, I would have the girls wash their hands in the bathroom and then assemble in the kitchen. On each occasion, I would always say, "Clean hands and a pure heart." It became so expected, that all I would have to say was "Clean hands..." and they would chorus in unison, "...and a pure heart." I was trying to emphasize to them that it was not only important to have clean hands for cooking, but to have at all times a pure heart on the inside as the Bible teaches in Psalm 24:3-4. *"...who may stand in His holy place? He who has clean hands and a pure heart..."*

Jesus also emphasized the importance of a pure heart in his Sermon on the Mount when he said, *"Blessed are the pure in heart for they shall see God."* (Matthew 5:8) As we studied in a previous lesson on pure motives, Jesus covered a lot of "heart" issues in the Sermon on the Mount. He was contrasting (and condemning) the outward show of religious practices and charitable deeds by the hypocrites with the same things done by a sincere, humble person with pure motives. As we learned from that lesson, it's what's inside that counts.

What's Inside?

When Saul was rejected by God as king of Israel, the prophet Samuel was given the task of anointing the new king. He was not told by God who it would be; he only knew that he would be chosen from among the sons of a man named Jesse. When Samuel saw Jesse's oldest son Eliab, he was impressed! He said, *"Surely the Lord's anointed is before Him."* (I Samuel 16:6b) Why did Samuel say this? What information was he basing this on? He was probably thinking of the appearance of King Saul and how he had stood out from all the others. **Read I Samuel 9:2.** How is Saul described?

_____

_____

_____

_____

138

Saul may have been tall, dark, and handsome, but his reign went south in a hurry when his heart was lifted up with pride and he rejected God. It is what cost him the kingdom and caused God to reject him and choose another to reign in his place. (I Samuel 15:26-28) As Samuel gazed at Eliab, maybe he saw the same impressive outward appearance. Perhaps Eliab was tall and strapping with a commanding presence about him. Samuel may have been impressed, but God was not. **Read I Samuel 16:7.** What does the Lord tell Samuel to ignore? _____

How does God see individuals? _____

_____

As you read through the books of I and II Kings and I and II Chronicles in the Old Testament, you will see an evaluation given for each king of Israel and Judah at the end of their lives. Read the following verses and note the name and evaluation of each king:

- **II Kings 14:23-24** _____

_____

- **I Kings 16:29-30** _____

_____

- **II Chronicles 25:1-2, 14-15.** _____

_____

- **II Chronicles 33:1-2** _____

_____

139

Jeroboam II was mighty militarily. He made war against the Syrians, recapturing cities and territories for Israel. King Ahab undertook extensive building projects, even accomplishing the architectual feat of building an ivory house. (I Kings 22:39) Amaziah was also a king of military might. He had a decisive victory over the Edomites, defeating them with a great slaughter and taking 10,000 of them captive. Manasseh of Judah had one of the longest reigns (55 years) and undertook extensive building projects as well as reinforcing the fortified cities of Judah. From all outward appearances, we might say these were powerful, successful kings, but God's evaluation of their reigns was entirely different. God was not concerned with their achievements, projects, or military victories. God looked at the spiritual conditions of their hearts.

Just as Samuel and the people of Israel were too focused on outward appearances, we are sometimes guilty of that as well, especially when it concerns ourselves. **Read I Peter 3:3-4.** What should our beauty *not* be based on? _____

_____

Does this mean we can't look nice on the outside? Not at all. Peter is simply saying that there is a beauty which penetrates far beneath the fine clothes, jewelry and cute hairstyles. It is that hidden person of the heart that wears a gentle and quiet spirit as her ornaments. This type of woman with a beauty that comes from within is *"very precious in the sight of God."*

Outward appearances are important, but they can be deceiving and hide a heart that is sinful. The Pharisees of Jesus' day were a prime example of this.

The Pharisees

When reading through the gospels, you will see many encounters between Jesus and a religious group called the Pharisees. You may notice that these encounters did not involve the exchange of pleasantries but tended to be harsh and severe.

The word "Pharisee" comes from the Hebrew word *persahin* which means "separate".[5] The Pharisees were a Jewish group that formed during the period between the testaments with the good intention of separating themselves from the pagan influences around them and strictly adhering to the law of Moses. The problem was that by the time Jesus walked this earth, this religious group had become full of pride and very hypocritical. They knew the law of Moses inside out and were looked to as the respected teachers and instructors of that law to the Jewish people. However, they were proud, boastful, and self-righteous and did not show compassion, mercy or love as the law originally contained and taught. They also added and enforced their own traditions, teaching them as doctrine to the people. (Matthew 15:3-9) Because of all of this, John the Baptist called them a *"brood of vipers"*

---

5   Easton's Bible Dictionary

in Matthew 3:7 and Jesus devoted a whole chapter to pronouncing woes against them in Matthew 23. Jesus explains the problem with the Pharisees in Matthew 23:3 when he says, *"Therefore whatever they tell you to observe, that observe and do, but do not do according to their works; for they say, and do not do."* Their inside did not match their outside. Let's read further to see what Jesus had to say about the outward vs. inward lives of the Pharisees.

Read Matthew 23. List some of the sins Jesus charges them with. _____

_____

_____

_____

Read Matthew 23:27-28. How does Jesus describe the Pharisees in these verses? _____

_____

You may have visited a cemetery that had some beautiful mausoleums on the grounds. They may have been made from sparkling white marble or polished stone with beautiful carvings and etchings on the outside, but the beautiful exterior does not change the fact of what is inside of them – dead bodies. A nice outward appearance on the Pharisees did not disguise their filthy and corrupted hearts from the Lord. Jesus says that outwardly the Pharisees looked good; they appeared righteous to everyone around them, but the Lord could see what was really going on in their hearts. What did Jesus say they were full of on the inside?

_____

_____

Jesus gives a similar description of them in the gospel of Luke. **Read Luke 11:39.** How does Jesus describe them in this verse? _____

_____

What did Jesus say they were full of on the inside?

_____

I have sometimes grabbed a coffee cup out of my cupboard that my dishwasher did not clean sufficiently. It looked perfectly clean on the outside, but when I took it off the shelf and looked inside, I saw dried residue from a previous beverage. Do you think I wanted to drink out of that cup? No way. I want a cup that is clean on the inside *and* outside. Jesus points out to the Pharisees that they would spend their time cleaning up the outside of their metaphorical cup or dish but totally neglect to clean the inside. In other words, they were useless vessels.

Neither passage in Matthew or Luke is complimentary to the Pharisees. Their outward show of righteousness meant nothing without a pure heart. No amount of putting on a good outward appearance will matter if it only goes skin deep.

You can fool many people most or even all of the time, but you will never fool God. The Lord is always looking at the heart of the matter.

God Is Searching...

Read Jeremiah 17:9-10. How is the heart described? _____

What is the Lord searching and testing and why? _____

_____

_____

Read Psalm 17:3a. What does David say the Lord is testing? _____

Read Psalm 139:23-24. In Psalm 139, David talks about how intimately God knows him, even to the very thoughts of his heart. He asks the Lord to search him and know him in verse 1 and to try him or test him in verse 23. What does David want God to examine him for in verse 24? _____

_____

David wanted to make sure that his heart was pure before God so that he could maintain a right relationship with him. There was a time in David's life when he keenly felt the separation that his sin had caused. After he was confronted with his sin with Bathsheba and involvement in the death of her husband Uriah, David penned the 51st psalm, his psalm of repentance. For months after the sin of adultery had occurred, David properly maintained his outward appearance of righteousness before the subjects in his kingdom, but his heart was not washed of the sin. Once he was confronted with his sin and the gravity of it, he knew he had to acknowledge his sin before God and ask for the cleansing of his heart. In verse 10, David prayed, *"Create in me a clean heart, O God, and renew a steadfast spirit within me."* Why did David long for a clean heart? **Read Psalm 51:11.** _____

_____

Sin separates us from our God. David fully understood this and prayed with a penitent heart for forgiveness, cleansing, and a restored relationship with the Lord. David realized that he could continue to offer sacrifices by the book, to sing praises as he strummed his harp, and to pray every day, but none of it meant anything to the Lord if there was not a pure heart behind the outward actions. **Read Psalm 66:18-19 and Isaiah 1:15.** If we are harboring sin in our hearts, what will God not acknowledge? _____

_____

Read Psalm 51:16-17. What does God desire?

_____

God has always desired our worship of Him to come from the inside out - from a heart that is pure, innocent, and sincere.

Conclusion

It is clear from the scriptures we have studied that we can put on an outward show of goodness and righteousness as the Pharisees did and as David tried to do, but in the end, it amounts to nothing if God sees iniquity in our hearts. Purity is equally important and necessary both inside and out.

For Thought or Discussion:

1. What is the importance of having *"clean hands and a pure heart"*?

2. Why was Samuel impressed with outer appearances? What are some modern examples of people being easily impressed with outer appearances to the exclusion of what's on the inside?

3. When and why did the Pharisees originate and how had they changed by the time of the New Testament?

4. List some of the sins the Pharisees were charged with by Jesus in Matthew 23.

5. As God searches your heart, what does He see?

6. Read Psalm 139:1-3. What does David say the Lord knows? What does the Lord *not* know about each one of us?

Challenge:

As you look at your own life, could you be described by Jesus as a white-washed tomb full of dead men's bones or a cup that is clean on the outside but unwashed on the inside? Strive to live your life with clean hands *and* a pure heart – from the inside out! Place a picture of a magnifying glass on your mirror. As you look at it each day, let it serve as a reminder that God is searching your heart.

Prayer Request:

Pray some of the scriptures we have covered in this lesson asking for a life that is pure inwardly as well as outwardly: *"Create in me a clean heart, O God, and renew a steadfast spirit within me,"* (Psalm 51:10); *"Search me, O God, and know my heart...see if there is any wicked way in me, and lead me in the way everlasting."* (Psalm 139:23-24)

Commit to Memory:

"Create in me a clean heart, O God, and renew a steadfast spirit within me." ~Psalm 51:10

Lesson 12: Godly Examples of Purity

At a recent memorial service for a dear sister in Christ, I was struck by the fact that more than one woman referred to her as their mentor. Sister Charlotte was looked up to and remembered for many things such as her world travel and sense of adventure, but it was her godly example that served as a role model for so many and it was that example that was mentioned over and over. She had a reputation for diligent service, genuine hospitality, and evangelism. I remember visiting her as her health declined and her energy waned. Her greatest frustration was not the aches, pains and bad days she experienced, but it was the fact that she could no longer do those things in service to her Lord as she had done for so many years. She was such a blessing to so many people, including me. Role models like Charlotte can be great if they encourage us in right, honorable, and godly living.

As women, we are fortunate to have many good examples in the Bible that we can look to for guidance in living a life of purity. Let's examine the qualities of the lives of three of these women: Ruth, Rebekah, and the Proverbs 31 woman.

Ruth

The story of Ruth takes place during the time of the judges of Israel. A severe famine in the land of Israel caused a man named Elimelech to take his wife Naomi and their two sons, Mahlon and Chilion, to the land of Moab to live. They lived there for about 10 years during which time Elimelech died. His sons married Moabite women, Ruth and Orpah, but both men soon died as well leaving three widows in the land of Moab. Being a widow in ancient times could be a very trying and terrible ordeal both socially and economically. When Naomi's husband died, she would have been dependent upon her two sons for support. When her two sons died, she faced an economic disaster. She could see no way to maintain a household for herself and her two daughters-in-law. She had heard that the famine was over in Israel, so her only hope was to return to her homeland and be dependent upon other relatives and the provisions given in the law of Moses for the care of widows. She loved Ruth and Orpah but realized they would be better off to return to their fathers' houses to be cared for and to possibly one day remarry. There was a tearful goodbye among the women, but only Orpah turned to go. Ruth clung to Naomi and would not leave her. We begin to see the bud of the beauty of Ruth as she does this, then we see it burst into full bloom as we read the touching words she says to her mother-in-law.

Read Ruth 1:16-17. Based on this passage, what are some words you would use to describe the character of Ruth? _____

_____

_____

Ruth's decision to go with Naomi would have been life-altering for her. Ruth was a Moabite and she was agreeing to leave her family, friends, and homeland for a foreign land where she would know no one except her mother-in-law. She was leaving behind her pagan gods and agreeing to follow the one true God. She was agreeing to take on the care and provision of her mother-in-law, knowing it would mean hard work for herself to feed them both each day. Considering all of this, Ruth still went. She loved and cared for Naomi so much, she was willing to do all of this for her at a great personal cost to herself. We see Ruth's love, loyalty, and total unselfishness on display through her decision to follow Naomi.

As Ruth and Naomi returned to the city of Bethlehem, the barley harvest had just begun. Ruth went to the fields of a kinsman of Naomi's named Boaz in order to glean and provide food for herself and Naomi. Gleaning was a process of gathering loose or leftover grain in the fields as the harvest was taking place. **Read Leviticus 19:9-10 and Deuteronomy 24:19-21.** How were the Israelites commanded in the law of

Moses to help provide for the poor?_____

_____

_____

_____

Boaz noticed Ruth as he came back from town later in the day and asked one of his servants who she was. What report did the servant give Boaz concerning Ruth? **Read Ruth 2:6-7.** _____

_____

_____

Ruth was evidently a diligent woman. She had been working hard all day as the servant had noticed.

Boaz was impressed with Ruth and showed extra kindness to her. He invited her to glean exclusively in his fields where there would always be plenty for her to gather and he put her under his personal protection. Ruth was surprised at such kindness shown to her because she was a foreigner. What reasons did Boaz give to her for his actions? **Read Ruth 2:11-12.** _____

_____

_____

_____

When Ruth returned from the field that day,

Naomi was impressed with the amount of barley she had brought home. Ruth explained about the kindness of Boaz and Naomi praised God for it. She was also thankful for the diligence of her daughter-in-law in working to provide for her. How long did Ruth continue to glean in the fields of Boaz? **Read Ruth 2:23.**

_____

Naomi was so grateful for all that Ruth had done, she wanted to see her married and provided for. Naomi had Boaz in mind as the potential groom. She knew he would continue to show Ruth kindness and provide for her as a husband. Naomi gave instructions to Ruth as to what to do. **Read Ruth 3:5** and note Ruth's response.

_____

_____

We continue to see the pure heart of Ruth in the way she treats her mother-in-law. We see her respect and obedience on display at this point. This was a big deal because Ruth is still a young woman at this stage of her life and Boaz is a much older man. Despite this, she is willing to trust and obey her mother-in-law and enter into marriage with Boaz. Boaz recognizes her sterling quality in this matter. How did he respond to Ruth? **Read Ruth 3:10.** _____

_____

Boaz could see how wise and unselfish Ruth was and he praised her for it.

As a result of Ruth's unselfish decision to follow her mother-in-law, she became the wife of Boaz and the great-grandmother of a very famous man in Israel. Who was it? **Read Ruth 4:13, 17-22.** _____

Rebekah

After the death of his mother Sarah, Isaac was sad and he was lonely. He was approaching the age of forty but had not yet married. His father Abraham, wanted his son to take a wife, but he didn't want just any woman for his son. They were living in the land of Canaan surrounded by pagan people who did not worship the one true God. Abraham wanted his son to have a wife from among his own people, his relatives. So he commissioned his servant to go back to the land of his people in Mesopotamia to find a wife for Isaac. To help ensure the success of this mission, whom did Abraham say would go before his servant? **Read Genesis 24:7.** _____

_____

When Abraham's servant arrived at his destination, he prayed for specific signs to help him identify the right woman for his master's son. **Read Genesis 24:11-14** to see what those signs were. As he sat by the well and waited, a young woman named Rebekah approached. She was the granddaughter of Nahor, Abraham's brother.

Read Genesis 24:16. How is Rebekah described?

_____

Not only was Rebekah beautiful outwardly but on the inside as well. She willingly served this stranger and went the extra mile for him by watering his camels. Unwittingly, she was fulfilling all of the signs which the servant had asked the Lord for in identifying the right wife for his master's son. Rebekah was clearly the chosen wife for Isaac.

She offered hospitality to this stranger in her father's home. The servant explained to her father the commission of Abraham, the requested signs from the Lord, and the apparent fulfillment in Rebekah. Rebekah's family realized that all of this was from the Lord. The only thing left was to ask if Rebekah was willing to go and marry Isaac. **Read Genesis 24:58.** What was Rebekah's response to this proposal?

_____

As Rebekah neared her new home, new husband, and new life, she saw a man in the distance out in the field. It was Isaac. Before he approached, Rebekah covered herself with a veil. The veil served as a token of modesty, respect, and submission. In that time and culture, unmarried women would cover themselves with a veil in the presence of their future husbands. Isaac and Rebekah were married and began their new life together. **Read Genesis 24:67.** What effect did Rebekah have on Isaac? _____

_____

Rebekah showed herself to be industrious,

hospitable, modest, respectful, and submissive. As a result, she was a fitting wife for Isaac and he loved her dearly.

The Proverbs 31 Woman

This woman is my role model and my hero. She is the woman I want to be some day when I finally grow up. She demonstrates every good quality that our heavenly Father wants his daughters to have. Whether it is in the area of marriage, motherhood, work, or service to others, she does it right. This passage in Proverbs is a description of everything a wise and godly woman should be. These qualities are described by King Lemuel's mother to her son as to what he should look for in a wife. (Proverbs 31:1,10) The Proverbs 31 woman is also referred to as the virtuous woman which is how verse 10 describes her. Some synonyms of virtuous are righteous, good, and pure.

Read Proverbs 31:10-31. List the qualities she possesses that apply directly to marriage. _____

_____

_____

_____

List the qualities that apply directly to motherhood.

_____

_____

_____

List the qualities that apply to work. _____

_____

_____

_____

_____

List the qualities that apply to service to others. _____

_____

_____

_____

The virtuous woman serves as an example of an excellent wife and mother. Her husband never has to worry that she is overdrawing the bank account or being idle. He knows she will never talk about him behind his back or put him down in front of others. He is confident in her abilities as a household manager and good mother to his children. He appreciates her diligence in her work as well as her compassion in serving the poor.

> He has no reason to be ashamed of her but on the contrary, he praises her for the excellent woman that she is.

She serves as a good example of a hard worker inside the home, outside the home, and in service to the Lord. This woman never lets grass grow under her feet! There is always something to do and she is busy doing it. She puts first things first and sees that all of the needs of her own household are met before tending to anything or anyone else. She puts her talents to good use in serving her own family and to help provide additional household income. With all that she has to do, she does not overlook the poor and needy but helps them all she can. She also gives the time and attention to her husband and children that they need and desire from her. Her children love and bless her.

We could sum up the qualities of the Proverbs 31 woman as virtuous, trustworthy, loyal, diligent, kind, compassionate, honorable, wise, shrewd, industrious, loving and faithful. What a great role model for all of us to follow!

Conclusion

A common denominator that these three women shared was faith. It takes faith to follow the Lord and to sometimes make difficult choices. It is what prompts us to live godly, pure lives and to have our priorities in the proper order. Let us each look to godly role models such as Ruth, Rebekah, and the Proverbs 31 woman so that we can learn to serve the Lord faithfully and model a godly life before others.

For Thought or Discussion:

1. Whom do you know that serves as a godly example of purity?

2. What characteristics does she (or they) possess that make her a good example to follow?

3. List some of the characteristics of Ruth. What do you admire most about her? What would you like to imitate in your own life?

4. How is Ruth described by other Jewish women in Ruth 4:15?

5. List some of the characteristics of Rebekah. What do you admire most about her? What would you like to imitate in your own life?

6. List some of the characteristics of the Proverbs 31 woman. What do you admire most about her? What would you like to imitate in your own life?

7. In I Timothy 4:12, who else does Paul say can serve as a role model and example to others in a faithful, pure life?

Challenge:

Think of other godly women in the Bible or your life who may serve as role models for you. Write down their names with a list of qualities they possess which you would like to imitate or enhance in your own life.

Be mindful that even as a young woman, there is

always someone younger watching you and looking up to you. Live your life in such a way that you can be a good role model to those younger than yourself.

Prayer Request:

Ask the Lord to keep good role models ever before you through His Word and in your life. Ask for strength and dedication to improving yourself and, if necessary, to make any changes needed in order to be a godly woman. Ask the Father to keep you mindful of others who may be watching you and to help you to encourage them in purity by the way you live your own life and to never do anything that might cause them to stumble in their walk with the Lord.

Commit to Memory:

"Charm is deceitful and beauty is vain, but a woman who fears the Lord, she shall be praised. Give her of the fruit of her hands, and let her own works praise her in the gates."
~Proverbs 31:30-31

Lesson 13: Maintaining Purity

We have seen through the lessons in this book what purity is, its purpose, and how it affects every area of our lives. We have also seen how vitally important it is to have a pure heart before God. As we close out this study, we want to end on a positive, hopeful note. This lesson will cover the why's of being pure, the how's of staying pure, and what to do if we have messed up along the way. (There is hope!)

Why You Should Be Pure

Let's examine ten Biblical reasons for being pure:

1) *You are set apart from the world.* **Read I John 2:15** and write it on the line. _____

   _____

   _____

2) *It shows that you respect yourself.* **Read Hebrews 13:18** and write it on the line. _____

   _____

   _____

3) *It glorifies God.* **Read I Corinthians 6:20** and write it on the line. _____

_____

_____

4) *You can draw near to God, and He can draw near to you.* **Read Psalm 24:3-5** and write it on the line.

_____

_____

_____

_____

_____

5) *You serve as an example.* **Read I Timothy 4:12** and write it on the line. _____

_____

_____

6) *Your body is God's temple.* **Read I Corinthians 6:19** and write it on the line. _____

_____

_____

7) *The pure in heart will see God.* **Read Matthew 5:8** and write it on the line. _____

_____

8) *It pleases God when you are pure; it is His will.* **Read I Thessalonians 4:1-3** and write verse 3 on

the line. _____

_____

_____

9) *You maintain a good reputation when you are pure.*
Read Proverbs 22:1 and write it on the line. ____

_____

_____

10) *You belong to God and as such, you are to be holy.*
Read Leviticus 20:26 and write it on the line. ___

_____

_____

How To Stay Pure

1) *Memorize God's Word.* **Read Psalm 119:11** and
write it on the line. _____

_____

_____

2) *Keep the commandments of God.* **Read John 15:10**
and write it on the line. _____

_____

_____

3) *Pray – ask for God's help when you are weak.* **Read
Matthew 26:41** and write it on the line. _____

_____

4) *Let the wisdom of God guide your decisions.* **Read James 1:5** and write it on the line. _____

_____

_____

5) *Watch what you watch.* **Read Psalm 101:2-4** and write the first part of verse 3 on the line. _____

_____

6) *Watch what you wear.* **Read I Timothy 2:9** and write it on the line. _____

_____

_____

_____

7) *Focus on God, not on sin.* **Read Hebrews 12:2** and write it on the line. _____

_____

_____

_____

8) *Just say "No!"* **Read Titus 2:12** and write it on the line. _____

_____

_____

_____

9) *Set good goals for your life that God will help you*

with. **Read Philippians 4:13** and write it on the line. _____

_____

10) *Guard your heart.* **Read Proverbs 4:23** and write it on the line. _____

_____

The Blessing of Hope

You may have studied through the lessons in this book and felt discouraged. Maybe you feel as if you have damaged your life in some way irreparably and can therefore, never be pure in heart.

Precious daughter of the King, let me assure you that our Father in heaven gives us one of the greatest gifts imaginable every day of our lives – the gift of hope.

So many times as I read through the pages of the Bible, I can see the bright beam of hope shining in the darkest of nights. At the very beginning of the Bible, in the book of Genesis, when Cain kills Abel, all hope of a Savior seems to die right along with him as the godly line appears to be snuffed out. What does God do next?

He blesses Adam and Eve with another son, Seth, whose name means, *"appointed"*. When he was born, Eve said, *"For God has appointed another seed for me instead of Abel, whom Cain killed."* (Genesis 4:25)

During the time of the judges of Israel, God's people went through a cycle of falling away from serving God faithfully and turning to idols; punishment from God in the form of disease, famine and oppressors; deliverance from their enemies; then finally turning back to God. This cycle occurred 7 times in about 400 years. Each time that God's people were in desperate straits and suffering due to their own sin, God gave them hope. He mercifully offered them a deliverer (a judge whom He would raise up) and would then use that judge to try to restore pure worship among the people.

During the time of the divided kingdom, God sent numerous prophets to warn the people to repent of their idolatry and turn back to God. Most of the time, the people refused to listen to these messengers of the Lord and He would then send calamities upon them to get their attention. In one such case, God punished the people with a plague of locusts which decimated the land and contributed to the starvation of the people. Destitute and stricken, the people of Judah may have wondered if this was the end. Could there possibly be any hope of survival or in the forgiveness of God? The prophet Joel delivered these comforting words to them: *"Now, therefore, says the Lord, Turn to Me with all your heart, with fasting, with weeping, and with mourning. So rend your heart, and not your garments; return to the Lord your God, for He is gracious and merciful, slow to anger, and of great kindness; and He relents from doing harm."*(Joel 2:12-13) As the rays of hope began to dawn in the hearts of the people, Joel continues in verse 21: *"Fear not, O land; be glad and rejoice, for the Lord has done marvelous things!"* What marvelous thing did Joel say the Lord would do for the people? **Read Joel 2:25a.** _____

_____

Not only was God willing to forgive, but He was ready to bless.

God desires to bless His people with hope. Even after the Jews had been exiled into captivity in the foreign country of Babylon for their sin of idolatry, God held out to them the gift of hope. He says through His prophet Jeremiah in chapter 29, verse 11, *"For I know the thoughts that I think toward you, says the Lord, thoughts of peace and not of evil, to give you a future and a hope."* Jeremiah tells the Jews that God will once again be found by His people when their hearts turn toward Him. He would one day bring them back from their captivity and gather them in their homeland. As a Jew in captivity, taken far from your home, seemingly driven from the presence of the Lord, and feeling hopeless, how would this revelation make you feel? Would your heart be full of thankfulness for the hope you could now cling to?

The apostle Paul is considered to be one of the greatest preachers, missionaries, and faithful followers of Christ. He is the author of almost half of the books of the New Testament and he boldly proclaimed the gospel to Jews, Gentiles, government officials, and kings. Yet, Paul called himself "the chief of sinners". (I Timothy 1:15) Why? **Read I Timothy 1:13.** What did Paul say he used to be? _____

_____

The man he was no longer existed. He was a new man in Christ. He recognized the mercy and grace that was offered to him through Jesus Christ and it changed his life. He experienced the blessedness of hope.

You say you can never make yourself pure? You're right, you can't, but Christ can! Jesus Christ our Savior is our blessed hope. He gave himself for each one of us to redeem us from every lawless deed so he can do what with us? **Read Titus 2:13-14.** _____

_____

_____

Hope is a motivating factor of purity. Why try to be pure? Because we have a hope in Christ and it makes us desire to be like him and to please him. **Read I John 3:3** and write it on the line. _____

_____

No matter what you have done in the past or what condition your life is in now, Christ Jesus offers his hope to you as well. If you are not a Christian but you believe in Jesus as the Christ, then repent of your sins and turn to God, confess him as the risen son of God and be baptized for the remission of your sins today (Mark 16:15-16; Acts 2:38; Galatians 3:27; I Peter 3:21). Become a new creature in Christ and walk in purity. God will be so excited, He will run to meet you! (Luke 15:20) If you are already a Christian, repent and turn back to God, praying for cleansing of your sins so you can once again stand clean and pure before your heavenly Father. God and His heavenly hosts are waiting to rejoice over your return. (Luke 15:10)

The beauty and blessedness of hope is that God always offers it. Each day that God gives you to draw breath on this earth, is another opportunity to wipe the slate clean and live for Him. One of my favorite book characters is Anne Shirley from the *Anne of Green Gables* series. She was notorious for getting into scrapes and making a mess of things. She would sometimes despair and just want to hide away from the world thinking she could never overcome her latest disaster. One day she was told something that became her new mantra and that has become a favorite quote of mine: *"Tomorrow is always fresh with no mistakes in it."* We don't even have to wait for tomorrow – God is giving each of us a chance this moment to start fresh. That is the embodiment of hope!

Conclusion

I pray that this study has blessed you and challenged you to grow purer in heart. Remember, you are a daughter of the King, a special treasure created by a God who knows you intimately and can wash you clean so that you may stand in His glorious presence.

"Who may ascend into the hill of the LORD? Or who may stand in His holy place? He who has clean hands and a pure heart..." (Psalm 24:3-4a) May the Lord God help each one of us to be purer in heart.

For Thought or Discussion:

1. List the 10 reasons why you should be pure:

2. Which one(s) challenge you the most and why?

3. List the 10 ways to stay pure:

4. Which one(s) do you honestly need to work on?
   What practical steps can you take to do better in
   any of these areas?

5. What does God always reach out to us with and
   why is it such a blessing?

6. What are some of your favorite scriptures or
   quotes about hope?

7. List every area of our lives that purity affects
   which was covered in these lessons:

Challenge:

Your final challenge is to be purer in heart. This is a tall order but one that you are up to. Desire to grow in your relationship with God, submitting every area of your life to Him. Loving God supremely and surrendering completely to Him will naturally motivate you to be pure as He is pure.

Prayer Request:

Pray for awareness of the areas in your life that need purifying. Humbly ask for forgiveness and cleansing. Humble your heart before God and pray for the wisdom and strength to have a heart that is truly pure before Him and displays itself to the rest of the world in order to glorify Him.

Commit to Memory:

"Blessed are the pure in heart, for they shall see God." ~Matthew 5:8

"Purer in Heart, O God"

Purer in heart, O God, help me to be;

May I devote my life wholly to Thee;

Watch Thou my wayward feet,

Guide me with counsel sweet;

Purer in heart, help me to be.

Purer in heart, O God, help me to be;

Teach me to do Thy will most lovingly;

Be Thou my Friend and Guide,

Let me with Thee abide;

Purer in heart, help me to be.

Purer in heart, O God, help me to be;

That I Thy holy face one day may see;

Keep me from secret sin,

Reign Thou my soul within;

Purer in heart, help me to be.

~Fannie Davison

About the Author

Heather Pryor was born in Ohio and currently resides in St. Petersburg, Florida. She has been married to her best friend and one true love, Paul, since 1988 and they have three children: Nicholas, Hannah, and Matthew. She has home-schooled her children all of their lives and has graduated all three.

Heather enjoys working with and mentoring children and young ladies, and teaching and encouraging women in the Lord. For seven years she directed a Keepers at Home club for girls aged 7-18. She now spends her time developing Bible curriculum and faith-based media products for home-schools, families and churches.

In her spare time, Heather enjoys baking, reading, cake decorating, drinking a good cup of Earl Grey tea, and spending time with her husband and kids.

Afterword

If anyone is interested in holding a Purity Banquet for young ladies and would like information on how to get started, please send a request to: Heather Pryor at <u>paulpryor@pryorconvictions.com</u> and type "Purity Banquet" in the subject line.

Made in the USA
Columbia, SC
24 October 2018